Personalities and Problems
Interpretive Essays in World Civilizations
Volume II

Personalities and Problems

Interpretive Essays in World Civilizations

VOLUME II

Ken Wolf
Murray State University

Illustrations by John Stephen Hatton

McGraw-Hill, Inc.

New York   St. Louis   San Francisco   Auckland   Bogotá   Caracas
Lisbon   London   Madrid   Mexico City   Milan   Montreal   New Delhi
San Juan   Singapore   Sydney   Tokyo   Toronto

This book was set in Palatino by The Clarinda Company.
The editors were Pamela Gordon and Joseph F. Murphy;
the production supervisor was Leroy A. Young.
The cover was designed by Circa '86.
R. R. Donnelley & Sons Company was printer and binder.

PERSONALITIES AND PROBLEMS
Interpretive Essays in World Civilizations
Volume II

This book is printed on acid-free paper.

1 2 3 4 5 6 7 8 9 0   DOC   DOC   9 0 9 8 7 6 5 4 3

ISBN 0-07-071347-2

Library of Congress Cataloging-in-Publication Data

Wolf, Ken, (date).
Personalities and problems
Includes bibliographical references.
1. Civilization—History.   2. Biography.   I. Title.
CB69.W63   1994   909   93-27176
    ISBN   0-07-071343-X   (alk. pbk.: v. 1)
    ISBN   0-07-071347-2   (alk. pbk.: v. 2)

About the Author

KEN WOLF is professor of History and coordinator of the Interdisciplinary World Civilization course at Murray State University in Murray, Kentucky, where he has taught since 1969. He was born in Davenport, Iowa, and received his B.A. degree from St. Ambrose College (1965) and his M.A. and Ph.D in History from the University of Notre Dame (1966, 1972). Professor Wolf helped design Murray State's required World Civilization course and has taught it since its inception. He also teaches German History and Development of Historical Thinking on a regular basis. Professor Wolf has published articles on European nationalism, historiography, intellectual history, and the teaching of history in *The Journal of the History of Ideas, The International Encyclopedia of Social Sciences—Biographical Supplement, Teaching History,* the *Illinois Quarterly,* and *The Journal of Kentucky Studies.* An article on teaching history through the use of biographical studies will appear in 1994 in the *AHA Perspectives.* For five years (1987–1991), Professor Wolf served as one of two deans of the Kentucky Governor's Scholars Program, a state-sponsored summer enrichment program for 700 high-achieving, rising high school seniors. He was selected as a Pew Faculty Fellow in International Affairs for 1993–1994. He is married with three children, Kevin, Christine, and Rebecca. His wife, Deanna, is a social worker.

To My Family (Deanna, Kevin, Cris, Becky)
and
To the Students, Faculty, and Staff of
the Kentucky Governor's Scholars Program,
1987–1991

For helping me give meaning
to the phrase "life-long learning."

Contents

Preface

Dear Reader:

The people you meet in these pages illustrate the richness and variety of human history over the past five centuries. The personalities range from the Portuguese adventurer, Prince Henry, to the twentieth-century Russian physicist and political activist Andrei Sakharov. One explored the oceanic frontiers; the other worked on the frontiers of modern Physics. If history is the study of human beings who make it, *Personalities and Problems* is an introduction to world civilizations which focuses upon some of the most interesting men and women which the written records of these civilizations allow us to meet. This book assumes no previous knowledge of history; it does assume that the lives of exciting people have a certain magic which captures our attention across the boundaries of space and time.

But most of you know that history is more (sometimes less) than the study of interesting people. If all the interesting historical figures were included in our history texts, the books would be too large to carry, much less read. The people we choose to include in our histories must also be considered memorable or important—by someone. Whether great in the traditional textbook sense of the term or not, each of these personalities was included in this work because I found them interesting and thought their lives could help you better understand some of the issues which historians and other scholars have struggled with in their teaching, research, and writing. Before you can assess their importance for yourselves, it will be helpful for you to begin to classify or organize them.

Eleven of the people you will meet in these pages were rulers or political leaders—people such as Otto von Bismarck, Ito Hirobumi, Tecumseh, Alfred Hugenberg, M. K. Gandhi, and Ho Chi Minh. Another seven were primarily intellectuals (writers, thinkers, religious leaders); this list includes Martin Luther, Desiderius Erasmus, Nicholas Condorcet, George Sand, Harriet Beecher Stowe, Robert Graves, and Ernest Hemingway. You will also meet several explorers (Prince Henry and Zheng He) and two modern scientists— Edward Teller and Andrei Sakharov.

Putting people in such broad categories is, of course, only one way to describe them—and not necessarily the best way. For one thing, in history as in life, people have a way of breaking through our neat categories. Gandhi was a political leader who tried to exert a profound influence on the religious life of his people. Andrei Sakharov will be remembered at least as much for his political views as for his creation of the H-bomb. And most of those we call intellectuals were memorable precisely because they were concerned with religious, political, and social/cultural issues (Harriet Beecher Stowe's work falls into all three categories). In a larger sense, this book is interdisciplinary; its author is committed to the idea that whatever lines we might draw between subjects in schools, we cannot understand human beings adequately if we separate their political behavior from their religious beliefs, their social position, or their economic concerns.

A second way of classifying people is to ask about the nature and extent of the impact they made on their society. Some, like Otto von Bismarck and Golda Meir, were important because they reflected in their actions the dominant values of their society. Others, such as Luther and Sakharov, were significant because they challenged those dominant values. Occasionally we find people who both reflected the beliefs of their time and place and tried to change the way people thought about the world. The Chinese mariner Zheng He did not change the direction of Chinese history in the fifteenth century, but his voyages of exploration offer a fascinating look at what might have been. His counterpart, Prince Henry of Portugal, both reflected European attitudes toward overseas exploration and, by his work, helped Europeans become even more outward-looking. People like Erasmus and Stowe challenged people in their respective societies to live up to the standards they professed.

These are only two ways of classifying the personalities in world history. As you read these essays, I invite you to devise some of your own. Your determination of what makes an individual a success or a failure, admirable or deplorable, will be based upon your personal values. I ask only that you also consider the times in which these individuals lived as well as the problems they faced. If you consider both their problems and the values which they brought to bear in trying to solve them, you will begin the process of thinking historically. You will become historically minded.

To help you with this task, all of these personalities are presented to you in relation to a particular issue or issues which they had to face or which their careers raise for us—as thoughtful citizens of an increasingly interdependent world. These issues—noted by the questions which begin each essay—include such things as the role of religion as a social force, the problems faced by females in male-dominated societies, and the relative importance of money and personality when one is appealing to voters. Each personality is also paired with a contemporary who had to face a similar problem or deal with a similar issue either in the same civilization or country or in another one. These pairings are often cross-cultural and should help you understand that human problems really do transcend the boundaries of race, creed, or nation. When we begin to see that individuals as different as the German Otto von Bismarck and the Japanese Ito Hirobumi had to face similar problems in constructing a modern government, we can appreciate the fact that our history is world history and not only a history of individual nations or even civilizations.

Historical greatness, then, is not just a matter of how talented we are (or how lucky) but also a matter of when and where we live. History helps make us as surely as we help make history. If this book challenges you to think about just how and why this happens, it will have served its purpose.

Because this book does not assume any prior knowledge of history, or even prior college-level work, I use brackets [ ] to define terms which might be unfamiliar to a beginning student. You also should know that each chapter is designed to stand independently; chapters need not be read in order. You can start at any point and read in either direction, after checking with your teacher and the course syllabus, of course! Finally, if you or your teacher think that some personalities are left out who should be included or some are included who should be left out, please let me know by writing to me at the address listed at the bottom of page xvi. As you might imagine, it has been difficult to balance the three goals of this work: interesting people, important issues, and useful cross-cultural comparisons. If, God and the publisher willing, *Personalities and Problems* goes into a second edition, I would be pleased to receive suggestions of people who ought to be included or omitted. Your comments will be taken seriously.

Personalities and Problems would not have been written without the generous moral and financial support of my colleagues at Murray State University. A sabbatical leave provided by these colleagues and financial support provided by the Murray State Committee on Institutional Studies and Research gave me the time to complete the book. I am particularly grateful to Joseph Cartwright, who suggested and supported the idea; to students Albert Reid, Ann Henry, Nick Greenwell, Rick Jobs and Cheri Harper Greer, whose bibliographic work, notetaking, proofreading, and word processing saved me many hours; to current and former Murray State colleagues Charlotte Beahan, Bill Schell, Mel Page, James Hammack, Wayne Beasley, Joe Fuhrmann, Burt Folsom, Roy Hatton, Terry Strieter, Hughie Lawson, Ken Harrell, Roy Finkenbine, and other readers, at Murray State and elsewhere; to Robert Blackey, California State University at San Bernadino; Nancy Erickson, Erskine College; and Thomas Keefe, Appalachian State University for their helpful reviews; and to History Editor Pam Gordon at McGraw-Hill, who did excellent editing and knew when and how to be encouraging as well as firm when asking for revisions. I would also like to particularly thank John Stephen Hatton for rendering all of the text art. Finally, I appreciate the many teachers and students in the Interdisciplinary World Civilizations course at Murray State who "field-tested" these essays in their classes over the past ten years. Any errors which you find are my responsibility and should not be blamed on any of the above, who often tried unsuccessfully to save me from myself. All of my colleagues do join me, however, in hoping that this work offers you both pleasant reading and intellectual excitement.

Sincerely,

Ken Wolf

Department of History
Murray State University
Murray, KY 42071

Personalities and Problems

Interpretive Essays in World Civilizations

Volume II

CHAPTER 1

Prince Henry and Zheng He: Sailing South

How do the structures and values of a society affect the way people view economic and political expansion and contact with other cultures?

It somehow doesn't seem fair. Prince Henry of Portugal (1394–1460), who was land-bound, is known to history as Henry the Navigator while the Chinese admiral Zheng He (ca. 1371–1435), who commanded fleets with hundreds of ships, is remembered as a eunuch, if at all. Of course, Henry's personal ability to navigate—if he had any—is not what made his life significant. Zheng He's condition as a eunuch [castrated male] did not affect his ability to lead men or manage fleets. Each man is remembered as he is because of the conditions and values of his society. These conditions and values also helped to determine how the Chinese and Portuguese reacted to the voyages of their remarkable explorers.

Between 1405 and 1433, the emperors of the Ming dynasty (1368–1644) created a fleet and ordered it to make seven expeditions into the "Great Western Sea," or Indian Ocean. The man selected to command these voyages, the most ambitious in Chinese history, was born Ma He, a member of a Muslim family of Mongol descent in the province of Yunan. When the first Ming emperor incorporated this Mongol province into his empire in 1381, Ma He was captured, castrated, and taken to the imperial capital of Nanjing, probably to serve as a harem guard. At age twenty, Ma He entered the service of the royal prince Zhu Di and very soon distinguished himself as a junior officer in a civil war that brought a new emperor to power. In 1404 the new emperor Yongle (reigned

1

1403–1424) promoted Ma He to the position of superintendent of the office of eunuchs and honored him with the Chinese surname Zheng. At about this time, the new head eunuch was described as tall and handsome, a man who "walks like a tiger and talks in a commanding voice."[1]

It was this commanding figure whom the emperor chose as leader of his new fleet. In this role, Zheng He's task proved enormous; he was to undertake seven voyages, each of which lasted nearly two years. On his first voyage in 1405–1407, he commanded 28,000 men on 317 ships, many of them large "treasure ships" 440 feet long and 180 feet wide. By contrast, Columbus "discovered" America eighty-five years later with 120 men and a fleet of three ships, one of which was seventy-five feet long. Zheng He's first expedition traveled to India, with stops at Java and Ceylon. The fourth expedition in 1413–1415 reached Aden and Hormuz on the Persian Gulf, and on the seventh expedition in 1431–1433 the Chinese sent a small group to visit Mecca; they also touched the east coast of Africa as far south as Malindi near the modern state of Kenya. At each stop, Zheng He presented lavish gifts to the local rulers from "their" emperor and recorded information about interesting customs and creatures he encountered. An "Overall Survey of the Ocean's Shores Annotated" was written by Zheng He's fellow Muslim Ma Huan; it was based on a diary that Ma Huan kept during the third, fifth, and seventh voyages.[2] Ma Huan's book shows the great interest the Chinese took in the dress, food, language, marriage and death rituals, and flora and fauna of the countries they visited. According to most modern historians of China, however, anthropological research was not the primary purpose of these costly trips.

There were a number of reasons why the court of the Son of Heaven initiated these voyages, discounting for the moment the exuberance of a young ruler and a natural curiosity about his neighbors to the south and west. To consolidate his power won in a civil war, the emperor decided to send what the Chinese called tribute missions to all neighboring countries to set up diplomatic exchanges. Owing to their advanced civilization, the Chinese, like other people before and since, believed that all other cultures were inferior and that once foreigners became familiar with Chinese culture they would realize it was the source of all wisdom and political power. While some representatives of foreign states felt the Chinese claim was unwarranted, many kowtowed [bowed] before the emperor either because they regarded it as appropriate, or because it enabled them to establish trade relations with the Chinese. Zheng He's voyages, then, were part of the Yongle emperor's effort to strengthen his own power by strengthening and expanding the tribute system. The voyages were also designed in part to curb Japanese piracy along the eastern coast of China, to check on possible Mongol activity in western Asia, and to search for treasure and overawe a few "barbarians." Zheng He accomplished these aims in visits to at least thirty-seven countries, many more than once. At the end of his fourth voyage in 1415, he brought back the envoys of thirty states to do homage to the Chinese emperor.[3] He also brought back a giraffe and a zebra to astonish the court; this latter creature, whose Swahili name sounded similar to the Chinese word for unicorn, was celebrated at court as a good omen for the dynasty and as an "emblem of Perfect Virtue, Perfect Government and Perfect Harmony in the Empire and in the Universe."[4] Zheng He's work had clearly boosted Ming prestige as well as increased Chinese trade with south and west Asia.

Therefore, from a Western perspective, it is surprising that the voyages of Zheng He were abruptly halted in 1433 and never resumed. Zheng He himself died several years after his last voyage. The exact date of his death, like that of his birth, is uncertain. After this, the Chinese went back to fighting nomads on the northern land frontier, something they had done for centuries. Japanese pirates soon reappeared along the southern coast. Zheng He's name lived on as the name of a Buddhist temple in Thailand and as the name of a well in Malacca.[5] In China, however, Zheng He and his travels to the "Western Ocean" were soon forgotten. A generation after his last voyage, an official in the Ministry of Defense even burned the log books of the expedition, whether deliberately or by accident, whether at the command of the emperor or on his own, no one seems to know.

We do know that a far different fate awaited the work of Prince Henry of Portugal, a man who became a legend in European history. Born in 1394 as the third son of King John I and Queen Philippa of Portugal, Henry became famous as the man whose sailors explored the west coast of Africa during the first half of the fifteenth century. Every grade school student knows that without the pioneering explorations of Prince Henry the Navigator, Bartholmew Dias would not have been able to round the Cape of Good Hope in

1487–1488, Vasco da Gama would not have sailed to India and back in 1497–1499, and Columbus would not have sought a sea route to the Indies in 1492.

Although he never personally navigated any ships south, Henry did make it his life's work to send out ship after ship from his rocky outpost of Sagres on the Atlantic coast of Portugal. Henry either outfitted the ships himself or granted a license to private captains who would repay him with a fifth of everything valuable they brought back. In the early years, when his ships were hugging the African desert lands, Henry usually spent far more than he earned. Although his ships were much smaller than those of Zheng He, Henry's record was impressive for his time and place. Men working under his direction settled in Madeiras and discovered and settled the Azores and some of the Cape Verde Islands. In 1434, Gil Eanes finally sailed beyond Cape Bojador on the west coast of Africa after Portuguese sailors had refused or been unable to do so on fourteen earlier trips. Many men feared sailing too far south. Current rumors included the belief that anyone passing Cape Bojador would turn black, that the sea boiled in the tropics, and that the sun's rays descended in the form of liquid fire as you approached the equator. Once the Portuguese passed Cape Bojador, a barrier more psychological than physical had been breached.

The Portuguese caravels [light, fast, maneuverable ships that could be sailed inshore] continued their journeys south in the late 1430s and 1440s. Alfonzo Goncalves Baldaia went 300 miles beyond Bojador in 1435, and in 1441 Nuno Tristao went down as far as Cape Blanco, halfway between Sagres and the equator. It was in this decade that Cape Verde was rounded, although it was not until the year of Prince Henry's death in 1460 that Pedro de Sintra reached Sierra Leone. In the early years, Henry constantly had to urge his sailors "to go back and go further." It was easier and more profitable to pirate Muslim vessels in the north than it was to take the more fearful route southwest along the barren desert coast. However, after several blacks were brought back to Portugal as slaves in 1441, the number and willingness of Henry's sailors grew. The slave trade and African exploration became intertwined, and Henry built the first European trading post used for slaves on Arguin Island in 1448.

While Prince Henry did not set out to secure slaves, the new trade in human beings did not trouble him greatly. Slaves had souls that could be saved and that appealed to Henry as much as did the selling and civilizing of them. Unlike his Chinese counterpart, whose voyages had no religious aims at all, Henry had a strong desire to spread his faith and fight the infidel Moors [Muslims in northwest Africa]. Zheng He, a Muslim, made no attempt to offend the religiosity of those he encountered. Personally, he offered sacrifices to a Chinese sea goddess before each voyage, but on a tablet he placed in Ceylon in 1409 with inscriptions in Chinese, Persian, and Tamil, he offered thanks to Buddha, Allah, and the Hindu god Vishnu—all of whom were worshipped on that island. Writing such an "ecumenical" inscription would have been literally unthinkable to Henry of Portugal. Indeed, his early interest in west African exploration was stimulated by the Portuguese conquest of the Muslim city of Ceuta on the north African coast in 1415; in 1437 Henry and his brother Fernando unsuccessfully attacked the city of Tangier, near Ceuta in Muslim Morocco.

The word "crusader" has medieval associations that contrast with our image of Henry as one of the first modern explorers, but the objectives of Henry the Navigator make him a crusader in the typical Iberian fashion. A major objective of his African expeditions was to "get behind" or outflank the Moors by sea. Like other medieval Christians, he had heard about the legendary Prester John, a Christian king in Africa somewhere south of the Sahara. If the Portuguese could reach Guinea, as they called black western Africa, they might be able to find an ally who could attack the infidel Muslims from the south. His desire to secure military allies contrasts sharply with Zheng He, who sought only tribute, information, and the opportunity to present gifts.

Although his explorations failed to secure Henry's military or diplomatic objectives against the Moors, they provided new geographical knowledge that improved future mapmaking and encouraged further Portuguese exploration. They also allowed him to promote trade and increase Portugal's political power at Spain's expense by controlling many Atlantic islands. In sum, Henry the Navigator's program mixed religion with politics in a way designed to appeal to the various components of Portuguese society. His brother, King Duarte I, supported Henry's work by granting him several royal monopolies. These gave him a fifth of everything of value brought back from south of Cape Bojador and made him the "landlord" of the Madeiras, the Azores, and Cape Verde. Henry also held the monopoly on all fishing and coral gathering along the Atlantic and Mediterranean coasts of Portugal and received all fees paid by fishermen to fish in these areas. He was reputed to be the "richest man in Portugal" after the king, but he probably died in debt because of the money he spent on exploration. The Portuguese merchants supported Henry's work because of the potential profits to be gained from exploration and the slave trade. Even Portuguese pirates were pleased by the opportunity his work gave them to raid and plunder under the cover of "exploring." The Catholic Church supported Henry's missionary efforts to convert the heathen and fight the infidel, and the aristocracy generally liked both the idea of crusading and the idea of increasing Portuguese power. The loyal peasants, we must assume, enjoyed Portuguese greatness vicariously, as most peasants in most places enjoy most forms of greatness.

Because of the broad-based support for Henry's work that existed within Portuguese society, he did not need to be a navigator. One modern historian, critical of the myth of Henry as a nautical genius who ran a "school" for geographers and sailors at Sagres, put the matter quite simply: "Henry harnessed his own talents and energies to those of his family and country. He did not need to invent ships, train sailors, educate pilots or give courage to his men. He found all these at his command. What he needed to do, and what he did, was to give focus to Portuguese energies."[6]

It was perhaps this as much as anything—the energies already there—that made the voyages organized by Prince Henry of Portugal the start of the "age of discovery and exploration" that we read about in our texts, while those of Zheng He, the Ming admiral, remained "mere exploits."[7] We should not forget the interesting similarities between Henry and Zheng He. Both sought power for their respective rulers, though in different ways. While neither favored outright conquest of the lands they explored, both found the idea of economic domination by the "mother country" acceptable. Both had sailing vessels suitable for long ocean voyages. Yet Henry's voyages marked a beginning and those of Zheng He an ending of maritime activity. Why?

One reason this question is so intriguing is that we have the benefit of hindsight. We know what came of the voyages of Prince Henry. We know how, in the words of one of his biographers, "he set a nation's steps upon a path that led to the world's end."[8] And we know as well what happened to China—and we wonder what might have happened. With their larger vessels and technical superiority (Chinese sailors had the magnetic compass in the eleventh century, perhaps two centuries before their European counterparts), would it have been that difficult for the Chinese to have dominated all of southeast Asia and established their power in India and even portions of Africa?[9] There was already a substantial overseas Chinese population in southeast Asia, and it showed every prospect of growing when the voyages were ended. If the Chinese had followed up on the voyages of Zheng He, what would the world be like today? They did not do this, of course. Instead China began to suffer from the intrusions of European sailors as early as the sixteenth century, just a century after Zheng He's voyages. China became prey to the West by 1850; it might have been Europe's strongest competitor. So much for speculation. What is certain is that the very structure of Chinese society in the fifteenth century made it difficult for Zheng He to be the pioneer that Henry was, even assuming that he wanted to be such a pioneer. Zheng He was a skilled administrator, diplomat, and seaman, but he was, above all, a servant of his emperor. His advancement in society depended on the emperor, not on any skills he might possess. There was little place in Ming society for a private or independent entrepreneur [risk-taking capitalist]. Trade was a government monopoly. The Son of Heaven employed servants such as Zheng He to do his will; he would never "contract out" exploration as the Portuguese king did.

There were also clear anticommercial and antiforeign biases in Chinese society during this time. The government got its money from taxes on land, not from taxing private traders and merchants. In addition, farming was considered more virtuous than business (as it was in medieval Europe until about this same time). Both Confucian and Christian ideologies glorified those who worked the land over those who soiled their hands with money. In the West, however, the diversity of states and their competition with each other as well as the perceived need for outside goods "from the East" stimulated the rise of capitalist towns and trade after 1150. The crusades of this century also helped break down traditional biases against commerce in Europe. China was more self-sufficient and thus faced no real pressure to change the traditional attitude toward either trade or outsiders.[10] The inhabitants of the Middle Kingdom (Ma Huan's translator calls it "the Central Country") did not look down upon outsiders because they were genetically programmed to do so; they did it because they could afford to: Their country was more prosperous than neighboring ones in the fifteenth century.

Given this, it is logical that the Chinese would simply view sea power as less important than maintaining a strong land army. It was. The chief threat to fifteenth-century China came from the northern barbarians; they, not Japanese pirates, were to overrun the country in the seventeenth century. All this means that both the Chinese and the Portuguese were quite sensible in choosing the course of action they did. There is nothing in the records, meager as they are, to suggest that Zheng He himself dreamed of a Chinese maritime empire. He may have, just as Henry may have wondered once or twice whether sailing down the coast of Africa would really defeat the Moors. Neither of these men of action spent much time pondering the consequences of their actions for future generations. That pondering they leave to us.

Notes

1. B. Martin and S. Chien-lung, "Cheng Ho: Explorer and Navigator," in *Makers of China: Confucius to Mao* (New York: Halstead Press, 1972), 112. Cheng, although his surname, is placed first in Chinese. [The new spelling of Zheng He used in this chapter represents the new Pinyin system of transliteration adopted by scholars only in recent years.]
2. Ma Huan, *Overall Survey of the Ocean's Shores Annotated*, edited and introduced by J. V. G. Mills (Cambridge: Cambridge University Press, 1970).
3. Jung-pang Lo, "Cheng Ho," in *Encyclopaedia Britannica*, 15th edition, *Macropedia*, Volume 4 (Chicago: Macmillan, 1974), 193–194.
4. Nora C. Buckley, "The Extraordinary Voyages of Admiral Cheng Ho," in *History Today* (July 1975), 468.
5. Ma Huan, *Overall Survey of the Ocean's Shores*, editor's introduction, 7.
6. Bailey W. Diffie and George D. Winius, *Foundations of the Portuguese Empire 1415–1580* (Minneapolis: University of Minnesota Press, 1977), 122.
7. Ma Huan, *Overall Survey of the Ocean's Shores*, editor's introduction, 34.
8. Elaine Sanceau, *Henry the Navigator: The Story of a Great Prince and His Times* (New York: Norton, 1947), 247.
9. Fernand Braudel, *Capitalism and Material Life, 1400–1800* (New York: Harper, 1973), 308, says that a Japanese junk, constructed much like those of Cheng Ho, traveled from Japan to Acapulco in 1610.
10. See Lynda Schaffer, "China, Technology, and Change," *World History Bulletin*, Volume IV (Fall, Winter 1986–1987), 1, 4–6; Paul Kennedy, *The*

Rise and Fall of the Great Powers: Economic Change and Military Conflict from 1500–2000 (New York: Random House, 1987), 8, notes that members of the Confucian ruling class (mandarins) distrusted merchants because they had less control over them. The mandarins hindered foreign trade by confiscating the property of merchants or banning their businesses on occasion.

Further Reading

BUCKLEY, NORA C. "The Extraordinary Voyages of Admiral Cheng Ho," *History Today* (July 1975), 464–469.

MA HUAN. *Overall Survey of the Ocean's Shores Annotated,* edited and introduced by J. V. G. Mills (Cambridge: Cambridge University Press, 1970). Exciting look at what fifteenth-century Chinese thought important.

SANCEAU, ELAINE. *Henry the Navigator: The Story of a Great Prince and His Times* (New York: W. W. Norton, 1947). Flowery hero worship in places but still useful and interesting reading.

CHAPTER 2

Erasmus and Luther: The Reformer's Dilemma

To what extent is it possible to reform an institution from within? What intellectual and personal qualities cause some individuals to be more radical than others, and what are the implications of such choices in history?

During the last two centuries of the European Middle Ages (1300–1500) people took religion more seriously than most of us can imagine. Bestselling books of the day "gave instructions, not on how to pay income tax, but on how to escape Hell."[1] This world, into which Desiderius Erasmus (1466–1536) and Martin Luther (1483–1546) were born, was one in which both heaven and hell seemed much closer to people than they do today. One reason was that life was shorter and more precarious for most people than it is for us.

Men and women heard stories of the Black Death, a plague which had carried off one-third of the population in many parts of Europe in 1348–1349, and which occasionally reappeared. They also experienced wars and famines that periodically swept through the countryside. Persons in the upper classes knew that princes and merchants gained and lost fortunes during these years as men fought to get their share of the new wealth coming from the East.

The Christian church, too, had to respond to this change and uncertainty. No longer as politically powerful as it had been in the thirteenth century, the church could no longer dominate kings and princes as it once had. And it could do little to control the plague or the economy. It could, however, take advantage of the longing for certainty of salvation which possessed many people in the days when Erasmus and Luther were growing up.

While Christian leaders found it difficult to explain why God had sent disease to bedevil men and women, they continued to comfort people with various forms of external piety to make them feel closer to God as they faced death from plagues, wars, or famines. Medieval Christians could assure themselves of God's favor (grace) and keep themselves in a "state of grace" (the opposite of a "state of sin") by undertaking any number of good actions, most of which cost time, money, or both. Clergymen encouraged the faithful to go on pilgrimages to holy places, usually shrines of saints, like that of Thomas Becket in Canterbury. Some princes and bishops also collected relics, usually portions of the bones or clothing of saintly individuals, which they were willing to allow people to view for a price. People could also pay a priest to say Masses for the salvation of their souls. Finally, one could receive an "indulgence," the remission of punishment for past sins, in exchange for specified prayers, and/or an offering of money to support a good cause. Indulgences could help a person escape all punishment for sins (in purgatory) and go straight to heaven after he or she died.

All these good works gave some comfort to those desperate for tangible evidence of earned "grace." They also helped enrich the institutional church which had control of their distribution. This "good works" theology, and the political power of the institutional church which lay behind it, offended the spiritual sensitivities of men like Erasmus and Luther who saw Christianity as a matter of inner devotion to Christ, and not primarily a matter of good works. These men, along with others, regarded the church as sorely in need of reform.

And it was reform of the church which they accomplished, though hardly in the way either preferred or imagined. Martin Luther sparked the famous sixteenth-century Reformation in 1517 when he wrote his famous list of "ninety-five theses" explaining errors in the church's policy on indulgences as preached by the German Dominican priest Johan Tetzel. In this statement, Luther asserted that God's free grace and not human works was responsible for our salvation. Luther was influenced by others, among them Desiderius Erasmus, a Christian humanist who suggested that true religion was much simpler and more Scriptural than the official church seemed to believe. After 1516, Luther prepared his university lectures and sermons using a copy of the Greek New Testament edited by Erasmus, whom he admired. After the Reformation began to divide most of Europe politically and religiously by the mid-1520s, it was said that "Erasmus laid the egg that Luther hatched," that Luther was merely taking to their logical conclusion some of the ideas of Erasmus. Erasmus denied this and, despite his early defense of Luther and his ideas, refused to reject the Roman church. Luther, by contrast, was excommunicated by the pope in 1520 and, in an act of public defiance, burned the letter of excommunication.

Both Erasmus and Luther were men who wished to improve the institutional church and the spiritual lives of its members. Their disagreements with each other—Erasmus deplored Luther's "violence" and the "tragedy" of a divided Christendom, while Luther denounced Erasmus as a coward and pagan who did not *really* understand Scripture after all—highlight the reformer's dilemma. Is it better to seek change from within an institution, even if you are likely to get less change that way? Or is it better to act boldly and accept the risk of getting expelled, as Luther was willing to do by 1520, in order to preserve your integrity and the opportunity to make more significant reforms? Is it better to promote greater change for fewer people, or less change for more people? Luther chose the first option; Erasmus the second. Their personal histories help explain their decisions.

By his own account, Erasmus of Rotterdam was born the bastard child of a priest on October 27, 1466.[2] Despite the circumstances of his birth, his parents cared for him well until their death from the plague when he was about fourteen. During his early years, Erasmus received a humanistic education at a monastic school in the Netherlands which stressed inward spirituality and devotion to Christ more that doctrine or dogma. This emphasis would remain a part of Erasmus's "Christian philosophy" throughout his life.[3]

Erasmus entered an Augustinian monastery at Steyn in 1487. Later he claimed he was ill with fever at the time and was "duped" into believing he could seriously pursue scholarship in the monastery. Erasmus took the religious vows of poverty, chastity, and obedience and was ordained a priest in 1492. He took the first opportunity, however, to leave the monastery, worked as secretary to the bishop of Cambrai for several years, and in 1495 began work on a Doctor's degree in theology at the University of Paris.[4] While in Paris, Erasmus found, as Luther did later, that he disliked the irrelevant "how-many-angels-can-sit-on-the-head-of-a-pin" sort of questions that preoccupied many medieval theologians. He did find himself attracted to the study of the ancient Greek and Roman virtues which occupied the attention of a group of men known as humanists. These scholars were involved in the intellectual movement known as the Renaissance and its revival of interest in classical learning, beginning in Italy about 1300 and spreading north during the next three centuries. During his student years in Paris and a visit in 1499 to England, where he met the famous Renaissance humanists John Colet and Thomas More, Erasmus evolved a synthesis of classical virtue and Christian piety which he felt could be used to reform the lives of individual Christians and thereby the church itself. From such pagan authors as Cicero he took the virtues of *humanitas* [love of mankind based on a belief in the dignity of man as a rational creature] and *concordia* [a rational harmonizing of conflicting viewpoints]. From Christian writers such as Jerome and from Scripture, Erasmus took the virtues of compassion, patience, forgiveness, humility, and love.[5]

Armed with his new convictions about the relationship between holiness and "good letters" or scholarship, Erasmus began to promote his beliefs. In an early work, *The Handbook of the Christian Soldier*, written in 1501, Erasmus argued that accurate knowledge of Scripture was extremely important to a Christian, and that religion was primarily a matter of inward devotions, love of God, and love of neighbor. In his witty, direct, but abrasive style, Erasmus wrote:

> You venerate saints; you are glad to touch their relics. But you condemn what good they have left, namely the example of a pure life. . . . You wish to deserve well of Peter and Paul? Imitate the faith of one, the charity of the other—and you will . . . do more than if you were to dash back and forth to Rome ten times. . . .[6]

To make the new learning possible for more Christians, Erasmus spent several years learning Greek so he could construct an improved edition of the New Testament from available manuscripts. This work, published in 1516, included a preface in which he wrote enthusiastically about his hope that someday God's word would be available to all. Christ's teachings were simple enough, he believed, that all men and women should have access to them in their own languages. "We embellish a wooden or stone statue with gems and gold for the love of Christ. Why not, rather, mark with gold and gems . . . these writings which bring Christ to us so much more effectively than any paltry image?"[7]

While some considered these judgments of Erasmus, by now a famous scholar, irreverent and perhaps even heretical, his attacks on the misuse of power by church leaders, their exaggeration of the trivial, and their ignorance were continuous and very deliberate. In his commentary on the New Testament, he would occasionally stretch a point to make the text apply "to the familiar targets of his criticism, the corruption of the clergy, the ignorance of the theologians . . . empty ceremonies, vows, penance, relics, and monasticism." Perhaps even more subversive was a satire which Erasmus wrote anonymously in 1513, *Julius Exclusus*. In this work, the warrior-pope Julius II is excluded from heaven by St. Peter because, instead of teaching "true doctrine," he has made the church "splendid with regal palaces, splendid horses and mules, troops of servants, armies, officers . . . glamorous prostitutes and obsequious pimps."[8]

Given the tone of many of Erasmus's criticisms of the church, it is not surprising that people would expect the Dutch humanist to be an early and enthusiastic supporter of the German reformer Martin Luther, since Luther and Erasmus criticized many of the same abuses. Such was not the case. From the beginning, Erasmus's support of Luther was hesitant and qualified; it soon turned to bitter disappointment. To understand why this happened we must understand that Luther's attack on the church came from a theological rather than a humanistic direction. "Erasmus was concerned about ignorance, Luther about sin," one author wrote.[9] The fact that Luther changed forever the religious map of Europe shows which of the two concerns most sixteenth-century believers took more seriously.

Not only sin, but life itself, was serious for the Saxon mining family into which Luther was born in 1483. His parents were strict and his early religious training a mixture of traditional piety and half-pagan beliefs in gnomes, fairies, sprites, and witches.[10] Like Erasmus, Luther had a sensitive soul, but grew up in a far less cosmopolitan environment. Perhaps it was to be expected that the young Luther, despite acquiring great learning in his later life, would spend many years seeking to be certain he was worthy of salvation.

For over fifteen years, Martin Luther sought that certainty of salvation by living as an Augustinian monk, a priest, and a teacher in the Saxon towns of Erfurt and Wittenberg. Luther was bright and energetic as well as earnest; he advanced far more rapidly than most after entering the cloister [monastic house] in Erfurt in the summer of 1505. Two years later he was ordained a priest, and five years after that, in 1512, he was made a doctor of theology, an honor usually given only those in their forties or older. By this time, Luther was professor of bible at the University of Wittenberg. One of his regular responsibilities was to preach and lecture to his colleagues in the cloister as well as to students. While preparing lectures on the Psalms and Paul's Epistle to the Romans, Luther experienced his great insight about faith.

Since he took his faith very seriously, Luther had been troubled for years by the feeling that no matter how hard he tried, no matter how carefully he performed his religious duties or confessed his sins, God remained angry at him. Luther struggled during these years to accept the fact that God did indeed love him. Sometime between 1512 and 1517, Luther had a "conversion experience." While reading Paul's words in the Epistle to the Romans "the righteous shall live by faith," Luther became convinced that nothing men or women can do can earn them salvation. People are saved by "faith alone" and not by any good or pious works.[11] This would become a central insight of the Protestant Reformation.

It was this basic insight, and the trust in Scripture which made it credible for him, which gave Luther courage to walk the road to Reformation. The first step on this road was the 1517 writing of the theses against doctrinal errors associated with the practice of granting indulgences. Though hindsight calls this the beginning of the Reformation, it was not immediately dramatic. More important were the events of the next four years: his debate with the theologian Johann Eck in 1519 in Leipzig, in which he denied the authority of the pope when it conflicted with Scripture; the pope's excommunication of him in 1520; and the meeting of the German princes at Worms in 1521, at which time he refused to deny his teachings and was declared an outlaw.

In addition, during the year 1520, Luther wrote three essays which, taken together, defined the major principles of Protestant or Reformed Christianity. In his *Address to the German Nobility*, Luther challenged the authority of the Roman pope in particular and the status of the clergy in general; he declared his belief in the priesthood of all believers. In *The Babylonian Captivity of the Church*, he attacked the sacraments as, for the most part, good works unjustified in Scripture. Eventually Luther and the Protestants reduced the sacraments to two, Baptism and Eucharist (Communion). Finally, in *The Freedom of the Christian*, Luther expressed his belief in salvation by faith. When the Elector of Saxony, Luther's prince, decided to protect him against the agents of the German emperor in 1521, it became clear that this theological rift had political overtones which might make it far less easy to heal than was apparent in 1517.

Back in Louvain (today in Belgium but then in the Netherlands) Erasmus was beginning to worry. He understood from the beginning of Luther's attack on indulgences that the German friar shared his dislike of external piety. Erasmus, however, disliked Luther's wholesale attack on church authority and his often strident language. (Luther called the Roman pope the "whore of Babylon" and the Antichrist). In a letter to Luther in May 1519, Erasmus suggested that "more can be accomplished by polite restraint than by vehemence." He also believed that "it is more advisable to scream out against those who abuse papal authority than against the popes themselves." To a mutual friend, however, Erasmus expressed his general support of Luther. "I pray," he wrote in July 1520, "that the supreme and wonderful Christ will so temper Luther's pen that he can be of very great profit to evangelical piety. . . . [Among] Luther's opponents I see many men who breathe the spirit of the world rather than of Christ."[12]

Erasmus's qualified support for Luther from 1519 to 1521 was based on their shared dislike of abuses and on the behavior of Luther's enemies. Rather than trying to prove Luther wrong from Scripture, as he challenged them to do, the Roman officials used authority: You cannot possibly be right because we have power and tradition on our side; if you do not recant, we will excommunicate you; we are not interested in the reasons for your position, just in whether or not you will stubbornly persist in holding to it. Writing to one of Luther's enemies, the archbishop of Mainz, in 1519, Erasmus said that "if [Luther] is innocent, I do not want him crushed by a faction of rogues, and if he is in error, I wish him to be corrected, not destroyed. This approach agrees better with the example of Christ." A year later, in November 1520, Erasmus met with Luther's prince, Frederick of Saxony, in Cologne. Frederick had asked for Erasmus's advice on the Luther question prior to the meeting with the emperor (Diet of Worms) to be held the following spring. Erasmus wrote a list of statements or axioms as guidance for Frederick. They suggested that the attack on Luther was caused "by the hatred of letters" and the "desire for supremacy." Erasmus added that those "closest to the Gospel teaching are said to be the least offended by Luther"; he noted that "this affair" should "be settled by the mature deliberation of serious and impartial men."[13]

But this would not happen. The papal letter condemning Luther was so violent that both Luther and Erasmus questioned whether it really came from the pope. It had. The declaration of the Diet of Worms making Luther an outlaw soon divided the German princes into two camps. Even in his 1520 axioms for Frederick, Erasmus had written prophetically: "The case is tending toward a greater crisis than certain men suppose." In succeeding years he continued to lament the "dangerous dissension" and the "tragedy" of the Lutheran affair. Several times he referred to the "bitter medicine" of Luther which, if swallowed, might produce good health in the church.[14]

For Erasmus the tragedy rapidly became a personal one. He was caught in the middle, with both sides insistently urging him to speak out on their behalf. For several years he continued to write critically about abuses in the church but refused to "join" the reformers in Germany or elsewhere because he believed one could correct abuses without leaving the Roman church. One did not have to attack papal authority, for example, in order to reform one's personal religious life in accord with the dictates of Scripture. Finally, in 1524, Erasmus did attack Luther's belief that man's will was so corrupted that without grace he could not do anything meritorious. To Erasmus's *Diatribe on the Freedom of the Will*, Luther responded in 1525 with his *On the Enslaved Will*. Although both men "talked past one another" in this debate, with each guilty of misunderstanding or exaggerating the views of the other, the exchange does illustrate the fundamental differences between the two reformers. Luther, in one of his extravagant and violent moods when he responded to the Dutch humanist, called him "a babbler, a skeptic, an Epicurean hog—stupid, hypocritical, and ignorant of Scripture."[15] There were clear temperamental differences separating these two reformers. Erasmus was a quiet scholar who could see nothing to be gained by loud shouting. Twice during these years,

he changed residences when the political temperature got too hot.
He left Louvain for Basel, Switzerland, in 1521 because of the anti-
Luther sentiment in Louvain. The tumult of the Reformation in
Basel drove him from that city in 1529 for five years. "I have seriously and openly discouraged violence," Erasmus wrote in 1524 to
his friend and Luther's close associate Philip Melanchthon. "Even if
I were an ardent devotee of the papist faction, I would still oppose
violence, because that path only leads to more violence."[16] He was
right, and there is nothing in his life to suggest he was not absolutely sincere on this point.

Yet there were also more than temperamental differences separating Erasmus and Luther—and these Erasmus did not fully understand. As early as 1517, after receiving Erasmus's New Testament translation, Luther wrote to a colleague that he was
suspicious of Erasmus's love of pagan learning. "I am afraid . . .
that he does not advance the cause of Christ and grace of God sufficiently," Luther wrote. This feeling that Erasmus somehow put
knowledge above grace continued to bother Luther in later years
and shows up clearly in the debate on free will.[17] Luther correctly
saw the differences between himself and Erasmus as theological. In
the words of Roland Bainton, the biographer of both men, they simply had different concepts of salvation: "This for Luther consisted
in the forgiveness of sins by a sheer act of God's grace, for Erasmus
in fellowship with God calling for a human response."[18]

Given this difference, all of Erasmus's talk about Luther's enemies really being enemies of "good learning," a theme that runs
through Erasmus's letters, is beside the point. So too is Erasmus's
belief that if only Luther and the Papists would lower their voices
and talk reasonably about the self-evident truth of Scripture, the
differences could be ironed out. Luther could not have done this,
even if he had been a calmer person less given to abusive language.
His God was simply not the one Erasmus worshipped. His God
was a demanding one, not interested in the rational moderation
stressed by many humanists. In the words of Bainton again, "the
God of Luther, as of Moses, was the God who inhabits the storm
clouds and rides on the wings of the wind. At his nod the earth
trembles, and the people before him are as a drop in the bucket. He
is a God of majesty and power. . . ."[19]

It is ironic that despite his differences with Erasmus, his strong
language, and his clear resentment of Roman abuses, Luther did

not see himself as a German nationalist and did not really want to divide the church. He called for "repentance and renewal" and was like Erasmus in simply wanting people to live virtuous lives based on Scripture.[20]

Yet the work of Martin Luther and, after him, John Calvin and others did bring about major changes in the Christian church. The Catholic bishops at the Council of Trent (1545–1563) reasserted their basic doctrines and made no attempt to accommodate the ideas of the reformers. Before long, Western Christendom was fragmented into hundreds of denominations and sects. Attempts to restore unity in dozens of bloody religious wars failed as Catholics and Protestants rejected the muted calls for a measure of mutual tolerance. It was common in that day to prove your love of God by hatred of your "heretic" or "papist" neighbor. It is only in our own day, a more ecumenical one, that some people have begun to better understand the real aims of both Erasmus and Luther and ask: "What if . . . ?"

Notes

1. Roland H. Bainton, *Here I Stand: A Life of Martin Luther* (Nashville: Abingdon Press, 1950), 29.

2. Desiderius Erasmus, *Christian Humanism and the Reformation: Selected Writings,* edited by John C. Olin (New York: Harper and Row, 1965), 23–25.

3. *Ibid.;* Roland H. Bainton, *Erasmus of Christendom* (New York: Charles Scribner's Sons, 1969), 8–11.

4. Erasmus, *Christian Humanism,* 26–27; J. Kelley Sowards, *Desiderius Erasmus* (Boston: Twayne Publishers, 1975), 4–9.

5. Bainton, *Erasmus,* 41–43, 113–114; Johan Huizinga, *Erasmus and the Age of the Reformation* (New York: Harper and Row, 1957), 102–103; E. Harris Harbison, *The Christian Scholar in the Age of the Reformation* (New York: Charles Scribner's Sons, 1956), 70–77.

6. Erasmus, *Christian Humanism,* 7–9.

7. *Ibid.,* 96–100, 106.

8. Sowards, *Erasmus,* 35–36, 88; Bainton, *Erasmus,* 106–109.

9. P. S. Allen, *Erasmus* (Oxford: Oxford University Press, 1934), quoted in Harbison, *Christian Scholar,* 110.

10. Bainton, *Here I Stand,* 22–23, 25–27.

11. John M. Todd, *Luther: A Life* (New York: Crossroad Publishing Co., 1982), 72–79; Bainton, *Here I Stand,* 60–66.

12. *Erasmus and His Age: Selected Letters of Desiderius Erasmus,* edited by

Hans J. Hillerbrand and trans. by Marcus A. Haworth, S. J. (New York: Harper and Row, 1970), 141, 149.

13. Erasmus, *Christian Humanism*, 138–139; 146–149.

14. *Ibid.*; *Erasmus and His Age: Selected Letters*, 153, 163, 177, 182; Bainton, *Erasmus*, 160.

15. Bainton, *Erasmus*, 187–190; Sowards, *Erasmus*, 103; one German theologian put Luther's position on free will (and indeed the general Protestant one) very succinctly when he wrote: "The central point of Luther's argument lies not in the question of whether man has the ability to do what he wishes, but rather in the question of whether he can do what he should." See Werner Elert, *Morphologie des Luthertums* (Munich: Beck, 1931), I, 22, quoted in G. C. Berkouwer, *Conflict Met Rome* (Kampen: J. H. Kok, 1948), 149.

16. *Erasmus and His Age*, 176.

17. *Luther's Works*, Volume 48, *Letters* I, edited and trans. by Gottfried Krodel (Philadelphia: Fortress Press, 1963), 40, 53; see Volume 49, *Letters* II (Philadelphia: Fortress Press, 1972), 44.

18. Bainton, *Erasmus*, 192.

19. Bainton, *Here I Stand*, 385.

20. See Heiko Oberman, *Luther: Man between God and the Devil*, trans. by Eileen Walliser-Sehwarzbart (New Haven: Yale University Press, 1989), 12, 44–46, 49, 64, 205.

Further Reading

BAINTON, ROLAND H. *Here I Stand: A Life of Martin Luther* (Nashville: Abingdon, 1950). Old standard work, very well done.

Erasmus and His Age: Selected Letters of Desiderius Erasmus, edited by Hans J. Hillerbrand and trans. by Marcus A. Haworth, S. J. (New York: Harper and Row, 1970). Gives reader a good look at the personality of Erasmus.

HUIZINGA, JOHAN. *Erasmus and the Age of the Reformation* (New York: Harper and Row, 1957). Sympathetic account by a fellow countryman.

TODD, JOHN M. *Luther: A Life* (New York: Crossroad Publishing Co., 1982). Thoughtful, fair work by a Roman Catholic.

CHAPTER 3

Kangxi and Louis XIV: Dynastic Rulers, East and West

To what extent can a dynastic ruler control his own fate? What is the key to successful "absolutism"?

In the world of the late seventeenth century, a comparison between Kangxi and Louis XIV is an obvious one. At opposite ends of the Eurasian land mass, these two rulers clearly stand out. In western Europe, Louis XIV (1638–1715), a member of France's Bourbon dynasty, ruled that continent's most powerful nation. In the far east, Kangxi (1654–1722), a member of the Qing dynasty (pronounced "ching"), was emperor of China.[1] Both rulers had equally long reigns. Kangxi's years of personal rule lasted from 1669 to 1722 (fifty-three years and four major wars) while those of Louis XIV extended from 1661 to 1715 (fifty-four years and the same number of wars).

Given their longevity, it is not surprising that each man experienced personal tragedies. Son and grandsons preceded Louis XIV in death, so that a five-year-old great-grandson, Louis XV, was left as successor in 1715. Kangxi's oldest son and "heir apparent" Yinreng was infamous for his acts of sexual depravity, sadism, and irresponsibility. After years of fatherly patience, sorrow, and cover-ups, Kangxi declared him mad and then deposed and arrested him in 1712.[2] These family problems were also political ones, for the success of dynastic government depends upon the quality of the ruler. In the Chinese case, Kangxi's fourth son, Yinzhen, proved to be a far more capable ruler than the original heir apparent would have been. The French were less fortunate: Louis XV proved to be a lazy and mistress-ridden monarch. The Qing dynasty lasted until

1911; the Bourbon dynasty collapsed in the storm of the French Revolution (1789–1799). The great energy and determination that both Kangxi and Louis XIV displayed clearly distinguish them from their successors. Kangxi's writings frequently note the importance of hard work and attention to detail. "This is what we have to do," he wrote, "[We have to] apply ourselves to human affairs to the utmost, while remaining responsive to the dictates of Heaven. In agriculture, one must work hard in the fields *and* hope for fair weather." Louis also relished the hard work necessary to run a large state. In notes he wrote for his successor, he warned against "prolonged idleness" and advised that a regular work schedule was good for the spirit; "no satisfaction can equal that of following each day the progress of glorious and lofty undertakings and of the happiness of the people, when one has planned it all himself."[3] Both rulers felt personally responsible for the welfare of their subjects, yet both fought major wars to extend their lands and their power. Since warfare was expensive in money and lives, it was not always easy for these men to balance their need for power with their desire to improve the lives of their subjects.

This very tension between war and peace helps illuminate some of the problems facing even a conscientious autocratic, or "absolute," ruler during these last few centuries before the world was transformed forever by the Industrial Revolution. Neither Louis XIV nor Kangxi had to please voters or make decisions about social and economic programs with one ear cocked to a national stock market or an international monetary system. Their job was simpler—in theory anyway. It was to strengthen the power of their dynasty by maintaining the military and economic strength of their country. The precise way in which each ruler pursued this goal tells us something about China and western Europe and something of the pitfalls facing an "absolute" ruler in the days before telephones and computers.

Kangxi was a Manchu. That fact defined his political task. The warlike Manchu nomads, who lived northeast of China, had gradually increased their territory and power at the expense of the Ming dynasty, which ruled China from 1368 to 1644. In the early seventeenth century, the Manchu leader Nurhaci (1559–1626) began to transform the Manchu tribes into a modern state by curbing the power of local chiefs and by centralizing the government. His sons continued this process of consolidation, and the Manchus were thus able to conquer Peking easily in 1644 once the last Ming emperor was defeated and committed suicide. The major problem facing Kangxi's father, who became the first emperor of the Qing dynasty, was to win support from native Chinese leaders, especially the Confucian scholars. To accomplish this he appointed two men to all top-level government positions, one a Manchu and the other a native (or Han) Chinese. Throughout his long reign, Kangxi continued this balance in making all major appointments so that native Chinese would not unduly resent their foreign leaders. This proved wise since the Manchus, while militarily superior to the Chinese in the beginning of the reign, were vastly outnumbered. To govern China successfully, a foreign dynasty had to have so much native help in ruling that it became virtually Chinese.[4]

Kangxi was only seven years old in 1661 when his father died, leaving the government to four noblemen assigned to govern on his behalf. Although Kangxi ended this regency in 1667, it was two years later before he was able to break the power of one particularly powerful regent. When the fifteen-year-old ruler acted, he did so decisively, throwing the offending overmighty subject, Oboi, into prison, where he died five years later.[5]

By acting decisively and wisely and by presenting a strong front to real or potential enemies, Kangxi strengthened his own personal power and that of his empire. His decision to maintain a strong army required that he increase its size from 185,000 in 1661 to 315,000 in 1684. To keep his troops sharp he also took up to 70,000 of them north of the Great Wall two or three times a year on hunting trips (really military maneuvers) so that they might practice archery and riding. Domestically, he supervised affairs in the provinces through loyal officials, many of whom were former Manchu army leaders who received appointments as provincial governors. In 1667 such appointees governed twenty-eight of the twenty-nine provinces. Kangxi also shrewdly conducted frequent audiences with military leaders; he believed that a general who bowed to the emperor occasionally would remain humble and "properly fearful."[6]

By the middle of his reign, Kangxi's wise choice of subordinates, realistic understanding of people, and close attention to detail reduced the danger of rebellion by unhappy Chinese subjects or discontented Manchu clan leaders. Before this happened, however, the emperor had to fight a bloody and prolonged war against three rebel leaders in the south. This war began in 1673 and lasted until 1682, in part because the emperor had trouble finding good generals. After defeating the three rebel states, Kangxi was able to add the island of Taiwan to his empire in 1684. It was more difficult to establish Chinese power firmly in the north. This took major campaigns against the Russians and against the Mongol chieftain Galdan.

Before moving to dislodge the Russians from Chinese territory along the Amur River where they had been settling since the 1650s, Kangxi made his usual careful preparations. He collected enough military supplies for a three-year war and moved Dutch-designed cannon and men trained to use them to the front. In 1685, he captured the Russian fortress at Albazin, and in 1689 the Treaty of Nerchinsk restored Chinese control in the area.[7] It took eight more years for Kangxi to defeat the western Mongol tribes led by Galdan. "Now my purpose is accomplished, my wishes fulfilled," the elated emperor wrote when a defeated Galdan committed suicide in 1697. "Isn't this the will of Heaven? I am so extremely happy!" These western victories set the stage for Chinese domination of Tibet, which began in the final years of Kangxi's reign and has lasted intermittently to our own day.[8]

Of course, external security was not enough. Dynastic rulers were obliged to keep constant and careful watch over subjects and subordinates. Kangxi did this by devising a system of palace memorials. These secret reports from agents of unquestioned loyalty to the ruler and the dynasty contained detailed information and comments, sent directly to the emperor and viewed by him alone. Their use allowed him to bypass official channels, to learn of official incompetence and would-be plots, and to quickly acquire more accurate information than that provided by the Grand Secretariat.

One of the emperor's most trusted agents was a Manchu bondservant named Cao Yin (1658–1712). This competent administrator had a classical Confucian education, and wrote poetry with his Chinese friends in his spare time; he was an ideal informant for Kangxi, who sent him to the city of Nanjing as textile commissioner in 1692. In his role as manager of imperial textile factories, Cao Yin supervised 2500 artisans and 664 looms, and he shipped quotas of silk to Beijing. In secret palace memorials written between 1697 and his death, he gave the emperor detailed information on the local harvest, problems faced by the local governor, and the "condition of the common people." Another secret memorialist sent reports to the emperor on the movements of 5923 grain boats that left Yangzhou for Beijing each year. Such information helped the emperor keep his officials honest and stop trouble before it started.[9]

Such close supervision of foodstuffs and silk production was important to a ruler who relied on a closely regulated economy. The textile factories at Nanjing, Hangzhou, and Suzhou were monopolies run by the government, which provided funds and established production quotas. During his reign, Kangxi tried to strengthen these government controls over trade. In 1699, for example, a statute ended private rights to purchase copper and gave the copper monopoly to merchants from the imperial household in Peking.[10] Neither Kangxi nor his French counterpart favored "free enterprise," which they considered inefficient and foolish. In their opinion the state alone had sufficient wealth to underwrite large commercial projects. These mercantilist rulers also asked why a private citizen should get rich with money that could be going to the state and ruler? They also worried that too-wealthy subjects might be more likely to support rebellion against their rule.

One of the central features of absolutist government was the clear tendency to link the welfare of a country with the power of its ruler. If this was the case in China, which enjoyed 2000 years of unified government, it was even more so for France. There, in the absence of a long tradition of dynastic government, it was often only the strength of the ruler that prevented the kingdom from breaking into the separate provinces from which it had been created. Louis XIV learned early the need for a strong monarchy; his lesson was as important in shaping French absolutism as Kangxi's Manchu heritage was in shaping Chinese government policies.

In 1648 when Louis was ten, an uprising known as the Fronde forced his mother and her chief minister, Cardinal Mazarin, to flee Paris to avoid capture by hostile armies. Although this uprising was poorly organized and sputtered within a few years, the revolt impressed the young monarch with the need to create both the image and the reality of a strong monarchy. When Louis assumed personal rule in 1661 after the death of Mazarin, he quickly established his authority by refusing to appoint a new chief minister and by arresting Nicholas Fouquet, his extremely wealthy and corrupt finance minister. By hard work Louis soon convinced others he was the "Sun King"; his palace at Versailles was soon the envy of other European monarchs.

The challenge Louis faced was greater than that which confronted Kangxi, since the former had to create a new tradition; the Manchu ruler, on the other hand, had only to prove that his new dynasty fitted into existing Chinese traditions. For centuries the French nobility had seen the king as only "first among equals." Louis had to change all that, and he did, using some of the same methods as his Chinese contemporary as well as some unique ones.

Like Kangxi, Louis employed officials loyal to him alone. But these differed from those in China, who were members of an ancient bureaucracy. Since France lacked a traditional bureaucracy, Louis had to build a new bureaucracy on the foundation laid by his father. His objective was to create an administration that allowed him to undercut the power of the old nobility while he strengthened his power at home and abroad. In selecting officials, the young king chose people from France's middle class—men of dedication and ability such as Michel Le Tellier as secretary of state for war and Jean-Baptiste Colbert as controller-general of finance. These commoners, like the Manchu bondservants used by Kangxi, had no social or political status other than that conferred on them by their employer; they were loyal servants because they owed everything to the king.

By employing them the king was able to create a civil and military organization that freed his dynasty from dependence on the old noble families of the realm. Louis's appointment of Colbert, in particular, proved judicious. As chief financial official, Colbert attempted to create a strong, state-directed economy designed to make the king strong in France and France strong in Europe. His international goal was a favorable balance of trade. So while the Chinese were producing silk for government consumption at state factories in Nanjing, Colbert was making France as self-sufficient as possible and generating income for the king by exports abroad from government-subsidized silk works at Lyons, linen factories at Arras, and pottery works at Nevers. To curb the import of foreign products into France, Colbert convinced the king to raise tariffs [taxes on foreign goods] in 1664 and 1667.[11] The adoption by France of this mercantilist economic system was based on the belief that there was only a limited amount of wealth in the world and the country that got to it first would prosper the most. Naturally

Colbert encouraged French establishment of trading colonies over-seas, and he strengthened the royal navy and merchant marine in order to make this sort of expansion more attractive. The limited success of Colbert's policies was due to their expense. The tax structure and its collection system could not generate enough revenue to meet military and civilian needs. The French farmed out tax collection to private citizens or tax farmers, who had to turn in a fixed amount of money to the king but could keep for themselves anything collected beyond that amount. Such a system encouraged graft and placed a great burden on the poor. The fact that Louis was unable to scrap this system in favor of one able to produce more revenue and greater fairness, and the fact that the nobility remained exempt from taxation, show some of the limitations on absolute monarchs in the seventeenth century.

That Louis used Le Tellier's professional army to engage in dynastic wars rather than using his limited funds to promote greater domestic prosperity shows another flaw in the system of absolutism. Dynastic wars reflected the will of a single person, and they served as the quickest path to necessary short-term prestige. Louis chose war, at first to secure glory and territory, and finally in self-defense. The War of Devolution, 1667–1668, was fought to get territory in the Spanish Netherlands (modern Belgium). It was a limited success but led to the less successful Dutch War of 1672–1678; the Dutch prevented a decisive French victory when they opened the dikes and flooded the territory around Amsterdam. The French did expand their frontiers in both wars, and they used dubious legal claims after 1678 to continue annexations along their eastern border, taking the important fortress city of Strasbourg (then in the Holy Roman Empire) in 1681.

All this, especially when combined with Louis's insufferable vanity (he offered to settle with the Dutch in 1672 if they would strike a gold medal in his honor thanking him for giving them peace),[12] naturally alarmed Louis' neighbors. When the king moved troops into Germany in 1688, he soon found himself facing a coalition of Germans, Dutch, and English. The War of the League of Augsburg lasted until 1697 and ended in a stalemate. Louis's last war, also fought against many enemies, was the War of the Spanish Succession, 1701–1713. The decision of the French king to place his grandson on the vacant Spanish throne threatened the "balance of power" in Europe by giving the Bourbon dynasty control of two major states. Louis made matters worse by refusing to promise that the two thrones would never be united. The "Sun King" was partly defeated this time. Like the earlier contests, this was a battle for overseas markets as well as political power, with the English fighting to capture French territories across the Atlantic as well as in Europe. The French did lose Nova Scotia and Newfoundland to the British in 1713 at the Peace of Utrecht. It was the prelude to further French defeats in the Americas later in the century.

In the final analysis, the wars of Louis XIV damaged his country and his dynasty as much as the wars of Kangxi had strengthened his. In Louis's defense, we should note that neither his armies nor his territorial gains were any greater than those of the Chinese emperor. His pursuit of glory and prestige was probably not as determined as that of Kangxi. The reasons Louis's absolutism was less successful than that of Kangxi are twofold: The Chinese absolutist system was much older and more firmly established than that of France; second, in the absence of strong neighbors the Chinese did not have to conduct foreign policy (the very term would have been foreign to Kangxi) in the midst of a system of rival states, each one concerned that none of the others become too strong. Kangxi did not have to establish a tradition of strong central government in the face of a hostile aristocracy. He had only to show that he, a Manchu, was fit to sit on the throne of the "Son of Heaven." In addition, Kangxi's foreign enemies were all inferior to him in strength. Finally, there was no "balance of power" in east Asia that the Chinese emperor was expected to maintain; China was the "central country" in east Asia in fact as well as in name.

All this is not to excuse Louis XIV's arrogance or errors of judgment. It was not a good idea, either politically or economically, for Louis to achieve religious unity by allowing his officials to persecute Huguenots [French Protestants] and in 1685 to revoke the Edict of Nantes, which had given them limited religious freedom. As a consequence, a significant number of Louis's most productive subjects fled to other countries, giving the king a bad image. Louis's splendid palace at Versailles did help him control the nobility by skillfully keeping them there in attendance on him. It also awed foreign monarchs and visitors. However, the "splendid isolation" of the dynasty outside of Paris alienated later Bourbon monarchs from their subjects and was one of the reasons for the collapse of the monarchy during the French Revolution. While the Chinese emperors might also be accused of "arrogance" by a Westerner (their court ceremonial, for example, was much more elaborate than that of Louis), their "arrogance" was sanctioned by centuries-long traditions. It was, we might say, an institutional rather than a personal arrogance. It is impossible, then, to evaluate the success or failure of either of these dynasts without taking into account their cultural and historical setting. For the Chinese, Kangxi proved a blessing. After fifty years of turmoil and inefficiency, he brought his subjects a long period of decisive, sensible, efficient rule. In short he proved himself a conservative restorer of the old.[13] Louis, on the other hand, while considered a conservative by modern standards (how else could a modern student of government view an advocate of one-man rule, sanctioned by God?), was revolutionary in the context of seventeenth-century French and European history. By identifying himself with the state, he helped to shift people's attention to the state as a focus for their primary loyalty.[14] His bureaucratic innovations, and even his wars, helped the French see their country as more than a collection of provinces. Louis may not get the credit for this, but he did help pave the way for the day when the French would die for "la patrie," the "fatherland." It is one of the ironies of French history that a chief victim of the new spirit of national unity Louis helped create was the Bourbon dynasty he had worked so hard to strengthen.

Notes

1. Kangxi (spelled K'ang-hsi in all but the most recent works) was his title, not his personal name. Chinese rulers, much like Roman Catholic popes, took a new name when they began their rule, and so Xuan Ye (this ruler's personal name) became *the* Kangxi emperor. Many historians simplify matters and avoid confusion by using the reign title or name as if it were a personal one. I do the same in this chapter.

2. Silas H. L. Wu, *Passage to Power: K'ang-hsi and His Heir Apparent, 1661–1722* (Cambridge: MA: Harvard University Press, 1979), is an excellent study of the "murderous power struggle" between K'ang-hsi and his son; see a good short summary in Jonathan D. Spence, *The Search for Modern China* (New York: W. W. Norton, 1990), 69–71.

3. Jonathan D. Spence, *Emperor of China: Self-Portrait of K'ang-hsi* (New York: Random House, 1974), 57; see also 11, 12–13, 47, 58–59, 147; Louis XIV, king of France, *Memoires for the Instruction of the Dauphin*, trans. with an introduction by Paul Sonnino (New York: Free Press, 1970), 29–30.

4. This process by which the Manchu dynasty became both powerful and Chinese is discussed in the first fifty pages of Lawrence D. Kessler, *K'ang-hsi and the Consolidation of Ch'ing Rule, 1661–1684* (Chicago: University of Chicago Press, 1976).
5. *Ibid.*, 65–73.
6. *Ibid.*, 105, 116–118; Spence, *Emperor of China*, 42–43. Governor-generals were military leaders who controlled more than one province.
7. Kessler, *K'ang-hsi*, 100–101.
8. Wu, *Passage to Power*, 65; Spence, *Search for Modern China*, 68.
9. Jonathan D. Spence, *Ts'ao Yin and the K'ang-hsi Emperor, Bondservant and Master* (New Haven: Yale University Press, 1966), 213–254.
10. *Ibid.*, 109–110.
11. Vincent Buranelli, *Louis XIV* (New York: Twayne Publishers, 1966), 72–78.
12. John B. Wolf, *Louis XIV* (New York: W. W. Norton, 1968), 224.
13. See Jonathan D. Spence, "The Seven Ages of K'ang-hsi (1654–1722)" in the *Journal of Asian Studies*, XXVI (February 1967), 205–211.
14. See Roland Mousnier, *Louis XIV*, trans. by J. W. Hunt (London: The Historical Association, 1973), 18–25.

Further Reading

SONNINO, PAUL (trans.). Louis XIV, king of France, *Memoires for the Instruction of the Dauphin* (New York: Free Press, 1970). Louis speaks for himself. Read with care.

SPENCE, JONATHAN D. *Emperor of China: Self-Portrait of K'ang-hsi* (New York: Alfred A. Knopf, 1974). Excellent. Brings this ruler to life.

WOLF, JOHN B. *Louis XIV* (New York: W. W. Norton, 1968). Long but readable.

CHAPTER 4

Burke and Condorcet: Are People Perfectible?

Are human beings perfectible, or are they fallen creatures who need to be controlled by their superiors? Can human nature and moral progress be understood through rational calculation?

It is a sign of the intellectual mood of the eighteenth century that this question, which most of us would consider private and religious, became public and political. After centuries, even millennia, in which the basic structure of government and society had been taken for granted, political thinkers such as Montesquieu (1689–1755), Voltaire (1694–1778), and Rousseau (1712–1778) began to earnestly and self-consciously wonder which form of government was best, and how to make governments more responsive to the needs of larger numbers of people.

But the thinkers of the eighteenth century did more than wonder. The last years of the century gave both Englishmen and Frenchmen the opportunity to implement some of their theories of government. In the 1770s the transplanted Englishmen in the North American colonies complained about "taxation without representation" and fought a successful war to free themselves from England and what they called the "tyranny" of English king George III. In 1787, guided by the ideas of European thinkers, the Americans designed a new republic with elected lawmaking bodies and a "Bill of Rights" to protect its citizens. Political rights—the right to vote and hold office—were limited to adult white males, who elected George Washington first president of this new United States of America in 1789.

In that same year, a more radical experiment began in France when the inept monarch Louis XVI called together representatives of each of the three Estates of the Realm (Clergy, Nobility, and Commoners) to deal with the bankruptcy of the French government.

The Third Estate (Commoners) soon took over and declared themselves a National Assembly. Within four years, the French created first a constitutional monarchy and later a republic; the king was executed in January 1793.

These two revolutions, and particularly the one in France which would result in a series of wars culminating with the defeat of Napoleon in 1815, led people to take more seriously words such as "liberty" and "equality." A centuries-old social structure, marked by a distinct aristocratic ruling class and an equally distinct group of lower and middle class "subjects," was collapsing. At issue was not only which form of government was best, but also how human nature should be understood.

The basic link between human nature and government was addressed most directly and dramatically at this time by two men, Edmund Burke (1729–1797) in England and Marie-Jean-Antoine-Nicolas Caritat, Marquis de Condorcet (1743–1794) in France. An English politician with nearly thirty years' experience in Parliament, Burke expressed his anger at the French revolutionaries in *Reflections on the Revolution in France,* written in 1790. Condorcet, a social philosopher, expressed his optimism about the future in his *Sketch for a Historical Picture of the Progress of the Human Mind,* written in 1793.

Both Burke and Condorcet were public men, as well as men of letters, who served their respective states for many years. Each had a consistent view of how people ought to be governed. Each looked to history to justify his beliefs, and each wanted humans to be as free as possible. Both opposed the tyranny of an unthinking electorate and that of an unchecked absolute monarch. The political and personal lives of both thinkers were marked by emotional struggle. Burke was a middle-class Irishman trying to succeed in the aristocratic political world of eighteenth-century England. Condorcet was an aristocrat who became a republican and voted to depose the king in 1792.

The central issue dividing these two passionate publicists is one which continues to intrigue many of us two centuries later: Are human beings perfectible on this earth? To this question, the violently antireligious "liberal" Condorcet answered yes; the traditionally religious "conservative" Burke said no. The question is deceptive because, while it can be answered briefly, the implications of the answer are far-reaching, and very divisive. A look at the lives and thought of these two men can help us see why this is so.

Born on New Year's Day in 1729 in Dublin of a Protestant father and a Roman Catholic mother, Edmund Burke was "pure Irish," in the words of one biographer. Although raised as a Protestant, his later sympathy for the Catholics in Ireland [who were then denied all political rights] may have been stimulated by his closeness to his mother; also, between the ages of six and eleven he lived with his mother's relatives. Burke received his college degree in Dublin before going to London to study law in 1750. Despite his father's wishes, the young man found traveling, coffeehouses, and debating clubs more interesting than legal studies. He lived this carefree life for a half-dozen years until his father cut off his allowance. Burke settled down in 1757; in that year he married Jane Nugent and published one of his first major literary works, an essay "On the Sublime and the Beautiful," a philosophical study of what constitutes beauty.[1]

Burke's lifelong interest in politics soon led him away from the literary career he had planned. From 1759 to 1765, he worked in London and Dublin for William Hamilton, chief secretary of the British government for Ireland. During this time, he wrote a tract against the "Popery Laws" which were used by the British to keep the Catholic Irish in the status of second-class citizens. After a disagreement with Hamilton in 1765, Burke became private secretary to the Marquis of Rockingham, leader of the mild opposition or Whig faction in the British Parliament. A seat in the House of Commons was arranged for Burke and he remained a member for nearly thirty years, retiring in 1794.

It was in Parliament that Burke made his reputation as an orator and supporter of limited government. In a 1770 essay on "Thoughts on the Cause of the Present Discontent," he argued against the attempt by George III to play a more active role in governing the country, and in a famous speech in 1774 after the Boston Tea Party, he urged Parliament to remove the duty on tea for the sake of peace with America and the preservation of the empire. One can picture the intense Irishman (contemporaries said he spoke quickly and with an Irish brogue) addressing these words to his colleagues:

> Be content to bind America by laws of trade; you have always done it. . . . Do not burden them with taxes; you were not used to do so from the beginning. . . . When you drive him hard, the boar will surely turn upon the hunters.

Burke believed that the English government did have the *right* to tax the colonies; it was part of the crown's sovereignty [right to govern]. But he warned that "if that sovereignty and their freedom cannot be reconciled, which will they take? They will cast your sovereignty in your face. Nobody will be argued into slavery."[2] Burke proved correct. The Americans put their practical needs ahead of their loyalty to the mother country. Because Burke had supported the Americans against George III's government and the Catholic Irish against the "Protestant Ascendancy," as the English rule in Ireland was known in those days, many were surprised when he argued so strongly in 1790 against the actions of the French revolutionaries. Had Burke lost his "liberal" spirit as he aged? Was he being inconsistent in supporting freedom for Americans but not for Frenchmen? Thomas Jefferson, for one, was "astonished" by Burke's views on the French Revolution, and suggested that it was evidence of "the rottenness of his mind." Even a more conservative John Adams agreed.[3]

But Edmund Burke had not become soft-headed in his old age, as these detractors thought. True, the language he used to describe the French revolutionaries in his *Reflections* was often intemperate, as when he described the revolution, then little more than a year old, as a "strange chaos of levity and ferocity . . . all sorts of crimes jumbled together with all sorts of follies."[4] Later in the book, he heaped exaggerated praise on the French queen, Marie-Antoinette, who had been forced by a mob to leave her palace at Versailles. Burke lamented that the age of chivalry was gone, and had been succeeded by one "of sophisters, economists, and calculators . . . the glory of Europe is extinguished forever."[5] As dramatic and romantic as this language is, it does contain some insight. Early on, Burke understood that the French were doing more than just remodeling their government a bit.

They were, in fact, changing the very basis of government. One of the first articles of their "Declaration of the Rights of Man and the Citizen," a bill of rights drawn up by the new revolutionary National Assembly in the late summer of 1789, stated that "all sovereignty resides in the nation." This was a genuinely revolutionary statement, for it suggested that the right to govern came not from God but from the people, not from above but from below. Long before many of his contemporaries, Burke sensed—perhaps intuitively

—what this would mean. Although the revolutionaries had not yet overthrown the monarchy when Burke wrote, their new abstract principles of government based upon popular sovereignty (or mob rule, as Burke called it) would allow them to make this change whenever they had the desire and the votes.

It also angered Burke that the French leaders were "atheists," a word he used frequently in the *Reflections.* They confiscated all church property in France in the fall of 1789 in order to provide security for the national debt. In Burke's view, this was immoral, illegal, and a bold attempt to destroy religion. Again here, despite his strident language, he had a point. The ideals of the French revolutionaries were profoundly secular; they wished to free people from "the chains of superstition" so that they could guide their lives by the rules of reason. The revolutionaries saw reason as something opposed to religion. Burke did not. Twenty years earlier, in 1769, Burke had written that "politics ought to be adjusted not to human reasonings but to human nature; of which reason is but a part, and by no means the greatest part."[6]

Although a reformer in the context of English politics, Burke wanted to base change on tradition. "A disposition to preserve, and an ability to improve, taken together, would be my standard of a statesman," he told the French.[7] Men's political rights, he argued, were established by prescription, that is, by long usage and custom. They could not be based upon some abstract rule of justice. Such changes as the French were making, and especially their replacement of aristocrats by middle-class commoners in the government, would subvert "the natural order of things."[8]

Burke's basic objections to the work and ideas of the French revolutionaries reveal more than his basic distrust of reason and abstractions. They show him to be a man with little faith in human nature. He admitted this at one point in the *Reflections* when he wrote:

> "We are afraid to put men to life to trade each on his own private stock of reason, because we suspect that this stock in each man is small. . . ."[9]

By the end of the eighteenth century, almost all political thinkers believed that people had certain rights. Burke and Condorcet, in fact, agreed that people had the right to justice, personal security, and protection of their property. It is interesting that Burke added to his particular list of rights, however, the right to have governments place "a sufficient restraint upon their passions."[10] Condorcet, while he agreed that men do not always act in their own interest, preferred to stress the duty of governments to enlighten rather than their obligations to punish. Where Burke was a pessimistic Christian, Condorcet was an optimistic atheist. This is one of the ironies we encounter in a study of the two men.

Another irony is that Nicolas Condorcet, an accomplished mathematician, was as "religious" in pursuit of his truth as Burke, the defender of tradition and history, was "empirical" [depending upon experience or observation alone] in pursuing his. Condorcet's intense hostility to religion is one of the most notable features of his political writings. This hostility may have been created in part by his very religious upbringing. After his father's death a month after Condorcet's birth, his mother—who had now been widowed twice—consoled herself by dedicating her young son to the Virgin Mary and dressing him in girl's clothes until he was eight. Condorcet was also educated by the Jesuits [a religious order of priests who had a reputation as good teachers but also as very scheming politicians].[11]

The young Condorcet's dislike of religion may also have been aided by his attraction to mathematics. At age twenty-two, he had an "Essay on Integral Calculus" published by the prestigious French Academy of Science, a body which admitted him to membership several years later in 1769. During these years, Condorcet was also the protégé [under the care and protection] of the famous French mathematician Jean d'Alembert. He showed great promise.

However, just as Burke was drawn from literature and philosophy into the world of politics, so too was Condorcet drawn from the study of mathematics into what one biographer has called "social mathematics." By the mid-1770s, Condorcet was becoming convinced that one could find the same kind of certainty in "the moral and political sciences" that one found in the physical sciences. After all, a century earlier Isaac Newton had discovered a mathematical formula which described the movement of the planets around the sun and the force of gravity. Was it not only a matter of time before we discovered laws which could make rational sense of the moral, social, and political behavior of people? To the quest for this "social science" Condorcet committed his life. He had faith that politics could be understood scientifically.

Since he believed that "to do good, one must have at least as much power as goodwill," Condorcet associated himself with Jacques Turgot (1727–1781), an economic and political reformer who attempted to strengthen the financial structure of the Old Regime [government of France before the revolution] during the mid-1770s. After Turgot was dismissed as controller-general of France in 1776, Condorcet continued his work, publishing an important "Essay on the Application of Mathematics to the Theory of Decision Making" in 1785. In this work he tried to show that one could use a calculus of probability to determine whether or not a given legislative body would produce what he called a "true" (i.e., enlightened) decision. Basically, his argument was that good people make good decisions, bad (i.e., unenlightened) people make bad ones. It is interesting that either despite or because of his belief in the value of mathematical abstractions, Condorcet was no more willing than Burke to let the uneducated mob rule. However, unlike Burke, Condorcet went out of his way to stress the importance of educating "the mob." He turned in a lengthy "Report on the General Organization of Public Instruction" to the French National Assembly in April 1792.[12]

After the French Revolution broke out, Condorcet's political activities became more direct. He was elected to the revolutionary legislative assembly in 1791 and was one of the first to declare himself in favor of a republic after he realized that King Louis XVI did not wish to cooperate with the revolutionaries. After the king was deposed in the fall of 1792, Condorcet soon found himself among the more conservative members of the new legislative body of the republic, called the Convention. He drew up a plan for a new constitution in February 1793. His plan, which would have provided for a system of representative government with universal male suffrage, was dismissed when his party (the Girondins) was replaced in midsummer by the more radical Jacobins.[13]

When the Jacobins took over the Convention, not only was Condorcet's attempt to create a "rational politics" ended, but he was soon ordered arrested when he attacked the new Jacobin constitution. It was during those last months of 1793, while in hiding in order to avoid execution, that Condorcet wrote his most optimistic and most famous essay, his *Sketch for a Historical Picture of the Progress of the Human Mind*. It is in this work, which begins with the bold assertion "that nature has set no term to the perfection of human faculties . . . the perfectibility of man is truly indefinite," that the differences between Condorcet and Burke become most apparent.[14]

Condorcet's *Sketch* was really just the outline for a much longer work that he was unable to complete before he left his hiding place, was arrested, and died in prison in March 1794. In this work, he planned to trace human progress through nine stages, running from earliest times to the beginning of the French Revolution. A chapter on the "Tenth Stage" was to describe "the future progress of the human mind." In each of the earlier stages of history, human attempts to make progress—usually defined in scientific or materialistic terms—had been stymied by greedy priests and despotic rulers, who used elaborate religious systems and sheer force to keep most people ignorant. It was only in the last few centuries before his own, Condorcet believed, that men and women began to throw off their prejudices and superstitions and become more rational, more willing to question authority and to think for themselves.[15]

It is in his description of the future that Condorcet becomes the most lyrical. "The time will therefore come when the sun will shine only on free men who know no other master but their reason; when tyrants and slaves, priests and their stupid or hypocritical instruments will exist only in works of history and on the stage," he wrote at the beginning of this chapter.[16] Condorcet expected that various kinds of inequality—in wealth, status, and education—would all be reduced if not eliminated. Medical discoveries would, he predicted correctly, lengthen human life. He also noted, again correctly, that the stock of human knowledge would increase, not because people would become more intelligent, but because they would learn how to measure facts and classify them more carefully. Condorcet announced that the future would see greater equality for women, and even something like what we call social security: "guaranteeing people in old age a means of livelihood produced partly by their own savings and partly by the savings of others who make the same outlay, but who die before they need to reap the reward."[17]

All this would happen, Condorcet was convinced, because people would continue, despite occasional setbacks, to apply abstract reason to the solution of human problems. Of course, it was just that use of abstract reason, in Edmund Burke's view, which caused the problems associated with the French Revolution in the first place. If the revolutionaries had not turned politics into an ideology [set of ideas] but had left it the art of working with people, there would be less pain in the world. If people like Condorcet were less intent on removing "prejudices" such as religion and instead were willing to learn from them, changes might come slowly but be more lasting.

Burke had his point, even if he did underestimate the abuses and errors of the royal government in France before 1789, and even if he was unwilling to admit that a concerted effort at social and political change can sometimes change things for the better (for example, the New Deal or the civil rights movement in the United States). But Condorcet also had a point, or rather a vision, which causes people to continue to read his *Sketch* to this day. If Burke anticipated the warnings issued by many twentieth-century political conservatives, Condorcet has been the patron of many reforming liberals. If Condorcet was naive in believing that moral progress could be made the subject of a calculus of probabilities, or that moral progress would necessarily follow from material progress—and he was—at least he put the accent on the improvement of people rather than on their control. That idea, even if wrong, has something uplifting about it.

If to Burke must go the award for common sense, to Condorcet must go the prize for hope. In the two centuries since the death of these men, many of those in public life have concluded that we need both of these virtues.

Notes

1. Philip Magnus, *Edmund Burke: A Life* (London: John Murray, 1939), Volume I, 6–12.
2. *The Works of Edmund Burke* (Boston: Little and Brown, 1839), Volume I, 489–490; see also Russell Kirk, *Edmund Burke: A Genius Reconsidered* (New Rochelle, NY: Arlington House, 1967), 62–65.

3. Isaac Kramnick, editor, *Edmund Burke* (Englewood Cliffs, NJ: Prentice-Hall, 1974), 125. The question of Burke's possible inconsistency in defending the Americans and not the French revolutionaries was raised again recently by the reviewer of a new biography of Burke. "How could the Burke who defended the right of the American colonists to defend themselves against the British government complain when the French tried to defend themselves against their government . . . how could Burke spend years trying to teach George III the limits of royal authority and now defend absolute monarchy in France?" See Alan Ryan, "Who Was Edmund Burke?" in the *New York Review of Books*, Dec. 3, 1992, 40; the essay reviews Conor Cruise O'Brien, *The Great Melody: A Thematic Biography and Commented Anthology of Edmund Burke* (Chicago: University of Chicago Press, 1992).

4. *Works of Edmund Burke*, III, 28.

5. *Ibid.*, 98.

6. Thomas H. D. Mahoney, editor, *Reflections on the Revolution in France* (Indianapolis: Bobbs-Merrill, 1955), xiii.

7. *Works of Edmund Burke*, III, 185.

8. *Ibid.*, 69.

9. *Ibid.*, 110.

10. *Ibid.*, 81; Keith Michael Baker, editor, *Condorcet: Selected Writings* (Indianapolis: Bobbs-Merrill, 1976), 73.

11. Keith Michael Baker, *Condorcet: From Natural Philosophy to Social Mathematics* (Chicago: University of Chicago Press, 1975), 3–4; see also J. Salwyn Schapiro, *Condorcet and the Rise of Liberalism* (New York: Harcourt, Brace, 1934), 66–67.

12. Baker, *Condorcet: Selected Writings*, x, xviii-xxii, 33–68; see F. De la Fontainerie, trans. and editor, *French Liberalism and Education in the Eighteenth Century: The Writings of La Chalotais, Turgot, Diderot, and Condorcet on National Education* (New York: McGraw-Hill, 1932), 323–378.

13. Schapiro, *Condorcet*, 129–133; Baker, *Condorcet: Natural Philosophy to Social Mathematics*, 316–330.

14. Marie-Jean-Antoine-Nicolas Caritat, Marquis de Condorcet, *Sketch for a Historical Picture of the Progress of the Human Mind*, trans. by June Barraclough (London: Weidenfeld and Nicolson, 1955), 4.

15. *Ibid.*, 99–172. Condorcet's titles are interesting. His "Eighth Stage" runs "from the invention of printing to the time when philosophy and the sciences shook off the yoke of authority." His "Ninth Stage" begins with the philosophy of Descartes (seventeenth-century French rationalist) and ends with "the foundation of the French Republic."

16. *Ibid.*, 179.

17. *Ibid.*, 179–193, 199.

Further Reading

BAKER, KEITH MICHAEL. EDITOR. CONDORCET: SELECTED WRITINGS (Indianapolis: Bobbs-Merrill, 1976). A good look at the variety of his work.

CONDORCET, MARIE-JEAN-ANTOINE-NICOLAS CARITAT, MARQUIS DE. *Sketch for a Historical Picture of the Progress of the Human Mind,* trans. by June Barraclough (London: Weidenfeld and Nicolson, 1955).

KIRK, RUSSELL. *Edmund Burke: A Genius Reconsidered* (New Rochelle, NY: Arlington House, 1967). Sympathetic account by a modern conservative thinker.

KRAMNICK, ISAAC. Editor. *Edmund Burke* (Englewood Cliffs, NJ: Prentice-Hall, 1974). Various views of Burke in his day—and later.

CHAPTER 5

Toussaint and Tecumseh: Resisting the Odds

Two leaders try to resist those who would enslave or exterminate them. Did either have a chance of succeeding? What legacy did they leave for us?

The nineteenth century was the great age of Western imperial expansion. Rich new lands had already been discovered and partially explored by white Europeans in Africa, Asia, and the Americas. Bolstered by their superior technology and their belief in a "civilizing mission," Western countries extended and tightened their economic and political control over lands occupied by races they considered inferior. By the end of the century the industrialized nations of the northern hemisphere dominated much of the rest of the world with a series of colonies, territories, and "spheres of influence."

Yet the path of conquest and control was not always a smooth one. Despite inferior weapons and faint hopes of success, native leaders often resisted the white conquerors. Occasionally a superior leader among the nonwhite peoples was even able to defeat or temporarily delay the conquerors. Toussaint L'Ouverture (1744–1803) and Tekamthi (1768–1813), whose name was later spelled "Tecumseh" by whites to make it easier to pronounce, were two such men.

Between 1792 and 1802, the ex-slave Toussaint created an army of blacks and mulattos [persons of mixed race] which dominated Hispaniola, a Caribbean island with a French colony in its western half and a Spanish one in its eastern half. His defeat of English, Spanish, and French armies sent against him in the French colony of Santo Domingo led to the establishment of the independent black nation of Haiti in 1804, a year after his death. A year later the Shawnee Indian warrior Tecumseh began his attempt to unite the Indian tribes in the Ohio and Mississippi river valleys of North

America. His seven-year effort to create an Indian confederation to prevent further seizure of Indian lands ended with his death in 1813 during the War of 1812 between Britain and the United States. Both men are remembered as brilliant military leaders and humane statesmen. Both were seen as worthy opponents by those who fought against them. While neither was able to ensure the prosperity of his people, each proved to be a shrewd political leader. Toussaint and Tecumseh left to their respective peoples a legacy of achievement and hope; each had a vision of freedom and racial harmony which transcended their place and time.

Visions of freedom were in short supply among the slaves of Santo Domingo when the great French Revolution broke out in the mother country in 1789. By that date, nearly one million Africans had arrived, imported to labor on the 800 sugar plantations. Although the slaves outnumbered the white masters ten to one and the mulattos seventeen to one, their death rate was much higher. Since many slaves were killed for sport or worked to death, the colony had to import large numbers of Africans (40,000 in 1787, for example) to keep the slave population at full strength.[1]

Despite the fact that his mother was a slave, Toussaint was better off than most members of his race. His father was a free man, educated by Christian missionaries, who gave Toussaint the opportunity to learn to read and write; he also mastered a few Latin phrases which he later repeated to the amazement of his troops. His education allowed him to become a house slave, which guaranteed him better treatment than that given field hands.[2]

It was clearly the reaction by the white planters to the French Revolution's extension of political rights which gave the oppressed blacks their opportunity for revolt and Toussaint his chance for leadership. In 1790, the colonial planters were given the right to govern themselves through a colonial assembly. The planters sought to deny political rights to mulattos, although the mulattos owned about a third of the land and a quarter of the colony's slaves. In response to their protests, the French National Assembly in May 1791 confirmed the rights of mulattos in the colony to vote and hold political office, but the French planters suspended that decree. As a result, the mulattos organized their own army and began a civil war. Both sides in this struggle ignored the blacks until a major slave revolt broke out on August 22, 1791, near the city of Le Cap François in the northern part of the island. When the white planters persisted in their refusal to grant limited rights to both blacks and mulattos, they lost their chance to control their fate; their world "collapsed under the weight of their own vengeance."[3]

The new Republican French government then attempted to salvage the situation in this economically important Caribbean colony by appointing a new governor and sending three commissioners from France to assist him in 1792. The most powerful of the three, Leger Felicite Sonthonax, was as hostile to the objectives of the promonarchist planters as the planters were to the objectives of the colony's blacks and mulattos. Unlike Toussaint, he failed to realize that he needed planter support to avoid the total collapse of the island's economy. Sonthonax supported first the mulattos, then the blacks; the state of near-anarchy worsened in 1793 when Spanish and British troops invaded the colony as part of their war against revolutionary France. Many white planters cast their lot with the British as a means of opposing Commissioner Sonthonax. Desperate for black assistance against the Spanish and British, Sonthonax abolished slavery on August 29, 1793.[4] This measure set the stage for Toussaint L'Ouverture, a shrewder and more racially tolerant man than either Sonthonax or the white planters, to play a major role in the Haitian Revolution.

Earlier in 1791, the gray-haired Toussaint had abandoned his position as a steward of livestock at the Breda plantation after having first helped his master's family find safety in Le Cap. He then joined the black rebels. Because he had organizational skill and could correctly assess the motives and abilities of others, Toussaint soon became a leader among the black insurgents and created a strong, disciplined army.[5]

In 1793 Toussaint and other black leaders joined the Spanish side in order to fight against their former French masters. But in May 1794, Toussaint made a crucial decision to defect to the French side. Some historians believe that he did this for both practical and idealistic reasons. Once the French National Assembly approved Sonthonax's abolition of slavery by its decree of February 4, 1794, it seemed logical to join the former enemy, especially since by this time virtually all the proslavery white planters had allied with the British. In addition, Toussaint realized he had little chance to rise to the top level of leadership with the Spanish because his way was blocked by two other black leaders, Biassou and Jean François.[6] Toussaint's decision proved a wise one. Within two years, his troops controlled most of the colony, and his territory was more unified than that controlled by the mulatto leader André Rigaud. Limited to territory in the southern part of the colony, Rigaud "kept whites in rigid subjection," whereas "for Toussaint, all colors were part of Saint-Domingue." By April 1796, Toussaint was appointed lieutenant governor by the French governor Etienne Laveaux, whom Toussaint had previously saved during a mulatto mutiny. By 1797 the black leader had a well-trained army of 20,000, the most powerful military force on the island.[7]

Once Toussaint defeated the British and Spanish and forced Sonthonax to sail for France in August 1797, he began to consolidate his personal power and to secure the political independence of the island. Although still technically subordinate to the French governor, Toussaint signed a treaty in May 1799 with the United States and the British who controlled the nearby island of Jamaica. In this treaty Toussaint guaranteed Jamaica and the southern United States against attack (US officials feared the slave revolt would spread) and received protection for his small navy. Armed with this new international respectability, he defeated the mulatto forces of Rigaud in August 1799. By summer 1801, Toussaint had merged the former Spanish colony on the island with his new country, had issued a new constitution, and had made himself governor-general for life. All this he did without permission from the French government, yet he claimed to remain a loyal subject. He did so in fear that revolutionary France would try to reimpose slavery when it had the chance.[8]

Toussaint's brilliant tactics were one reason for his great military and political successes. He was able to inspire his troops to march more than fifty miles in a single day over mountainous terrain; as a master of guerrilla warfare, he was able to strike without warning and then to disappear quickly into the mountains. But Toussaint L'Ouverture (his last name, added in 1791, meant "the opener") was also a clever judge of both his enemies and of what we call today "public opinion." He anticipated Sonthonax's proclamation to abolish slavery four days in advance and issued his own proclamation. In it he reminded slaves that freedom was not a gift confirmed by whites but rather a status which had to be earned with his help. In late 1796 when Sonthonax proposed to Toussaint that they establish an independent state, kill all whites, and make Sonthonax dictator, Toussaint responded with a grin: "And when I have declared my independence of France and have massacred the whites, what would the Commissioner advise me to do with him?" Several years later Toussaint told a friend that he was glad to have the emotional and vengeful Rigaud as his mulatto opponent. "Monsieur Rigaud," observed Toussaint, "lets go the bridle when he gallops. He shows his hand when he is about to strike. I gallop too, but I know how to curb. And when I strike people feel the blow, but do not see it coming."[9]

Toussaint's wisdom is also confirmed by his plans for the social and economic reconstruction of the colony. Toussaint astutely realized that many ex-slaves would seek to avoid field work if allowed and that the economy of the island would disintegrate if all the skilled white planters and mulattos left. To avoid this, he used military force to keep field hands on the plantations but guaranteed them collectively one quarter of the income from the plantations. The government also took over abandoned plantations and kept half of the proceeds, but made sure that the absentee proprietors received twenty-five percent of the profits. Toussaint also tried to maintain cordial relations with Britain and the United States, realizing how important foreign trade was to the welfare of his people.[10] All of Toussaint's policies, however, required two things which he knew he could not guarantee: racial peace at home, and the absence of foreign interference from abroad. That he was aware of these social and political realities is revealed in a comment Toussaint made to a white woman, who wanted him to grant her husband an official position and act as godfather to her son:

> Madam, God alone is immortal. When I am dead, who knows if my people will not again . . . pass under the yoke of slavery? . . . Man's work does not endure. . . . You wish me to appoint your husband? So be it! Let him be an honest man and remember that even if I can't see everything, wrong does not remain unpunished. As for becoming your son's godfather, I can't grant that request. The whites would blame you, and the time might come when your son would blame you too.[11]

Toussaint realized his achievements might be short-lived. Once Napoleon Bonaparte assumed control of France in November 1799, he decided to restore authority over France's colonial empire in the West Indies and reimpose slavery in Santo Domingo. Toussaint's power forced Bonaparte to move slowly, and it was not until 1802 that the first installment of 20,000 French troops arrived in the island. Jealousy among his military subordinates stymied Toussaint's plan to draw the French troops into the mountainous interior where they could be more easily defeated. Nevertheless, the French lost many troops to battle and yellow fever. For reasons which are still unclear, Toussaint, who failed to foresee the eventual defeat of the French, agreed to lay down his arms in May 1802. It is possible he did so in order to gain time for his troops to regroup. He also may have considered his army ultimately doomed in the face of superior French forces and the determination of Napoleon. In a brief memoir written after he was captured and sent to jail in France in the summer of 1802, Toussaint said he surrendered to preserve public order. Since this memoir was written to convince Napoleon to release him from jail, Toussaint's comments must be read with great caution.[12]

Two years after Toussaint's death in prison in April 1803, his Shawnee contemporary Tecumseh began his effort to unite North American Indians as Toussaint had attempted to unite blacks, whites, and mulattoes in Haiti. Tecumseh's effort was as determined as that of the black leader; it was also, in the last analysis, as unsuccessful.

Tecumseh, or "shooting star," was born in March 1768 in the Shawnee village of Piqua, situated in southern Ohio. The youth witnessed constant conflict between Indians and white settlers, and he developed a keen hatred for whites. When he was six, Tecumseh's father was killed fighting against Virginians. Two of his brothers were also killed by American settlers, and in 1780 an American army commanded by George Rogers Clark wiped out his native village and destroyed the crops. Two years later, a village of peaceful, Christianized Delaware Indians in eastern Ohio was destroyed and the people massacred in cold blood by frontiersmen. In response to these offensive acts, some sources say, Tecumseh's mother stirred him to take vengeance against the "enemies of his race," men whose "souls are dark in treachery and their hands red in blood."[13]

Like Toussaint, Tecumseh learned early that no single race had a monopoly on cruelty or virtue. Tecumseh befriended several white "foster brothers," children captured and raised by the Indians; he even lived with Daniel Boone when the famous Kentuckian was a captive of the Shawnee from April to June 1778. As a teenage member of a Shawnee war party, Tecumseh became angry when his comrades tortured and killed an innocent white captive along the

Ohio River. Throughout his life, he maintained that mistreatment and murder of captives was unworthy of a warrior. Tecumseh's biographers also generally note his kind-hearted treatment of the elderly, the poor, and the weak among his own people and among whites. His Indian and white contemporaries were impressed with his forcefulness and nobility. Some reported that he had "a marked sense of personal dignity" combined with "a hot temper and strong self-control." Tecumseh could command respect and use his anger effectively.[14] One American trader described Tecumseh as a man "fluent in conversation and a great public speaker [who] was hospitable, generous and humane—the resolute and indefatigable advocate of the rights and independence of the Indians."[15]

Despite his natural leadership abilities, Tecumseh did not begin his organization of the Northwest Indians until his early thirties. By that time, it had become clear that the whites would slowly push the Indians ever further west unless the Indians organized across tribal lines to stop them. A 1795 treaty with some tribes gave the United States government two-thirds of Ohio and a portion of southeastern Indiana. By that date Indian leaders were forced to abandon their hunting grounds in Kentucky, and settlements in the rest of Indiana were the obvious next goal of the whites. President Thomas Jefferson's administrative policy from 1801 to 1808 encouraged the Indians to farm rather than hunt (which required much more land), and those who refused or took up arms were forced across the Mississippi River. Meanwhile the supply of game animals in this area dwindled and many Indians, unable to supply their families with game and unwilling to take up farming, faced serious food shortages. The situation was worsened when whole tribes took to drink, imbibing large quantities of rum willingly supplied by white traders.

Aided by his brother Lalawethika, Tecumseh tried to halt this steady process of decline. In 1805, Lalawethika experienced a mystical religious conversion that turned this formerly lazy drunkard into the "Prophet." Changing his name to Tenskwatawa ("the open door"), Tecumseh's brother appealed to the Shawnees and to Indians of other tribes to stop drinking and to return to the traditional Indian ways of life. Tenskwatawa preached an antiwhite code of behavior. Stop marrying whites and wearing white men's clothing, he told his followers. The Prophet claimed to have supernatural powers given him by "the Master of Life" [God] which could help his followers defeat the white men in battle. Tecumseh hoped this religious revival could inspire his people to halt the white advances. He had long believed that Indian land belonged to all tribes and that individual Indian leaders had no right to sell parcels piecemeal to the American government. Tenskwatawa's appeal as a powerful holy man now gave him a new weapon to use in his effort to unify the Indians of the northwest and Ohio River valley against the Americans. In the following years, Tecumseh made a series of journeys through Indian territories from Wisconsin to Florida and as far west as Missouri and Arkansas to organize an Indian confederation. To help focus their movement, Tecumseh and the Prophet moved with many supporters to Greenville, Indiana, and, in 1808, to a new village along the Tippecanoe River in western Indiana. Alarmed by this Indian political and religious revival, William Henry Harrison, territorial governor of Indiana, countered it by poking fun at the new prophet and his followers. If Tenskwatawa was really a prophet with supernatural powers, Harrison scoffed, let him "cause the sun to stand still, the moon to alter its course, the rivers to cease to flow. . . . If he does these things," he told the Indians, "you may then believe that he has been sent by God." When he discovered that there was to be an eclipse of the sun on June 16, 1806, Tenskwatawa accepted Harrison's challenge and said he would make the sun darken on that day. Following appropriate ceremonies and before a large audience, the Prophet prayed and ordered the sun to disappear. Harrison's carelessness won many converts for Tenskwatawa that day.[16]

But the American settlers continued to flock west, despite Tecumseh and Tenskwatawa's best efforts to promote Indian unity. "These lands are ours; no one has a right to remove us, because we were the first owners," Tecumseh told an Indian council in 1807. "As to boundaries, the Great Spirit above knows no boundaries, nor will his red people know any."[17] Yet in the Treaty of Fort Wayne, signed in 1809 while Tecumseh was away on one of his recruiting trips, Harrison secured tribal agreement to abandon further territory to the United States. The new treaty helped Tecumseh recruit more Indians to his confederation during the coming year, but a face-to-face meeting between Harrison and the Indian leader in 1810 resulted in brave and angry words by Tecumseh but no political concessions by the governor. Late in 1811, while Tecumseh was again away seeking allies among the Choctaws and Creeks in the south, Harrison, fearing Tecumseh's growing power, defeated the Prophet's forces and destroyed the village at Tippecanoe.[18]

The battle of Tippecanoe was a turning point in Tecumseh's career. The "strong medicine" of the Prophet failed to work against Harrison's troops. Tecumseh was angry with his brother because he had wanted to avoid conflict until the confederation was fully organized. When he returned to stand upon the ashes of his former home, Tecumseh publicly humiliated Tenskwatawa, grabbing him by his hair and threatening to cut his throat. Then he vowed vengeance against the "long knives" for the attack.[19]

That vow of vengeance forced Tecumseh to lead his band of a thousand warriors to ally with the British in the War of 1812 against the Americans. Despite the fall of Detroit to the British in that year, the Americans greatly outnumbered their protagonists. Once Oliver Hazard Perry defeated the British on Lake Erie in September 1813, final American victory was certain. Tecumseh was angered at the British retreat east into Ontario after Perry's victory, but he followed, leading his braves into his final battle against his old enemy Harrison in the battle of the Thames on October 5, 1813. The fact that neither his body nor his secret grave was ever positively identified only added mystique to the legend of the Shawnee who dreamed of an independent Indian nation in North America.[20]

Tecumseh lived on in the imagination of the American people. Even Harrison saw fit to report to Washington that if Tecumseh had not had to fight the United States, he might have created an Indian empire which would have rivaled that of the Aztecs in Mexico or that of the Incas in Peru. One biographer called him "a man of extraordinary abilities and possibilities"; another called him "the greatest Indian."[21] Such praise should not obscure the fact that Tecumseh's dream of Indian unity was in fact impossible from the beginning. Many tribal leaders opposed his confederation because of jealousy or simply because such an idea was alien to their traditional ideas of tribal autonomy. Such opposition was apparent on his recruiting trip south in 1811. On that trip Tecumseh spoke to leaders of six great tribes, yet only the Muskogee and the Seminole leaders paid much attention to his pleas—and they only promised to consider his request for warriors. He had no firm commitments from the southern tribes at the time of the battle of Tippecanoe.[22] Even if Indians had joined him in large numbers, American settlers would have eventually used their numerical superiority to occupy the valuable agricultural lands of the midwest. The Indians were so outnumbered that any victories which they would have won on the battlefield would only have been temporary. Even those Indians who did turn to agricultural pursuits were believed to be racially inferior by whites and were soon pushed onto the least arable lands—eventually to Indian reservations in the western United States.

Although both Tecumseh and Toussaint relied on outside forces in an effort to achieve their goals, Toussaint achieved greater success in playing off the white nations against each other in Haiti than Tecumseh did by relying upon the British to defeat the Americans. Toussaint was at least able to end slavery in his homeland. After his death, the French were defeated and Haiti became an independent state. However, it did not become the country Toussaint wished it to be. His successors, Jean Jacques Dessalines and Henri Christophe, threw out the French and avenged Toussaint's death at the price of an antiwhite policy which turned Haiti into one of the most impoverished states in the western hemisphere. This social and racial policy was a betrayal of Toussaint's vision. At best, it enabled them to stir up the blacks to the extent necessary to obtain their personal and national freedom.[23]

Given this, can we still speak of the legacy of achievement, vision, and hope passed on by these two leaders? Certainly we can. In the first place, both Toussaint and Tecumseh were heroes to their people. One modern author sees the struggle by Tecumseh and the Prophet as the antecedent of the twentieth-century "Red Power" movement by Native Americans. Their noble pan-Indian effort failed, but it could be recalled with pride by their descendants.[24] In addition, Tecumseh's Indians, by joining the British in the War of 1812, may have played a crucial role in keeping the Americans from capturing Upper Canada [the area directly north of the Great Lakes] during the war. This could have resulted in permanent United States control of part of Canada.[25] Toussaint's struggle had a more direct effect on American territorial expansion. When the French lost the colony of Santo Domingo, Napoleon gave up his hope of creating a Western empire and decided to sell Louisiana to the Americans. Thomas Jefferson's Louisiana Purchase in 1803 virtually guaranteed that the new United States of America would become a continental nation.

Another reason for choosing to remember these men today, in a much "smaller" but still hostile world, is the vision of racial harmony which each man tried unsuccessfully to impart to his followers. While it may have been "good politics" for Toussaint and Tecumseh to promote harmony between the races, it is important that they opposed torture, murder, and mistreatment of captives and other innocent people of other races at a time when most people were willing to accept such excesses. In promoting racial harmony, as in their broader political struggles, Toussaint and Tecumseh resisted the odds against them, even among their own followers.

Any attempt to evaluate the achievement of these men, then, must take into account the way we choose to define greatness in history. "Great men make history," one historian wrote in evaluating Toussaint, "but only such history as it is possible for them to make. Their freedom of achievement is limited by the necessities of their environment."[26] A true test of historical greatness might require us to ask not only what a person has done but also how successfully a person was able to resist the odds against success. By that test both Toussaint L'Ouverture and Tecumseh have more than earned the few words they usually are given in most textbooks.

Notes

1. Ralph Korngold, *Citizen Toussaint* (New York: Hill and Wang, 1965; original, 1944), 11, 15, 33–34, 105–106.
2. *Ibid.*, 55–57.
3. *Ibid.*, 20, 55–57; Thomas O. Ott, *The Haitian Revolution, 1789–1804* (Knoxville, TN: University of Tennessee Press, 1973), 48–55.
4. Ott, *Haitian Revolution,* 65–72; Korngold, *Citizen Toussaint,* 103.
5. Ott, *Haitian Revolution,* 57–58; Korngold, *Citizen Toussaint,* 77–78; C.L.R. James, *The Black Jacobins: Toussaint L'Ouverture and the San Domingo Revolution,* Second Edition, Revised (New York: Vintage Books, 1963), 90–93.
6. Ott, *Haitian Revolution,* 82–83; Korngold, *Citizen Toussaint,* 105–106.
7. Ott, *Haitian Revolution,* 85–88; James, *Black Jacobins,* 181.
8. Ott, *Haitian Revolution,* 110; Korngold, *Citizen Toussaint,* 89, 118–119, 139.
9. Korngold, *Citizen Toussaint,* 99–101, 110–111, 129, 160.
10. Ott, *Haitian Revolution,* 130–134; Korngold, *Citizen Toussaint,* 130–131, 205–208.
11. Korngold, *Citizen Toussaint,* 150.

12. See Korngold, *Citizen Toussaint*, 284–297; Ott, *Haitian Revolution*, 160–161; "Memoir of Toussaint L'Ouverture," in *Toussaint L'Ouverture: Biography and Autobiography* (Boston: James Redpath, 1863; reprinted by Books for Libraries Press, Freeport, NY, 1971), 295–328.

13. Glenn Tucker, *Tecumseh: Vision of Glory* (Indianapolis: Bobbs-Merrill, 1956), 26–27, 46; Benjamin Drake, *Life of Tecumseh and His Brother The Prophet* (Cincinnati: Anderson, Gates and Wright, 1858; reprinted by Kraus Reprint, New York, 1969), 66–71; Alvin Josephy, Jr., "Tecumseh, The Greatest Indian," in *The Patriot Chiefs: A Chronicle of American Indian Resistance* (New York: Penguin Books, 1976), 137–141.

14. Albert Britt, "Tecumseh, The Shawnee Who Dreamed of Empire," in *Great Indian Chiefs* (Freeport, NY: Books for Libraries Press, 1969), 136–137; Tucker, *Tecumseh*, 30–32, 36–40, 67; R. David Edmunds, *Tecumseh and the Quest for Indian Leadership* (Boston: Little, Brown, 1984), 44.

15. Bil Gilbert, *God Gave Us This Country: Tekamthi and the First American Civil War* (New York: Doubleday, 1990), 194.

16. Tucker, *Tecumseh: Vision of Glory*, 99–101.

17. Drake, *Life of Tecumseh*, 93.

18. Josephy, "Tecumseh, The Greatest Indian," 160–161.

19. Tucker, *Tecumseh: Vision of Glory*, 230.

20. See Klinck, *Tecumseh: Fact and Fiction*, 200–230, for conflicting accounts of Tecumseh's death.

21. Gilbert, *God Gave Us This Country*, 5; Josephy, "Tecumseh, The Greatest Indian," 131–132.

22. Tucker, *Tecumseh: Vision of Glory*, 214–217.

23. Ott, *Haitian Revolution*, 189–191; Franklin W. Knight, *The Caribbean: The Genesis of a Fragmented Nationalism* (Oxford: Oxford University Press, 1978), 156–157.

24. Arrell Morgan Gibson, *The American Indian: Prehistory to the Present* (Lexington, MA: D.C. Heath and Company, 1980), 284–286.

25. For a look at the numerical weakness of the British and the strength of the Americans, see James W. Hammack, Jr., *Kentucky and the Second American Revolution: The War of 1812* (Lexington: University Press of Kentucky, 1976), 25, 32, 109–111. See also Gilbert, *God Gave Us This Country*, 329.

26. James, *The Black Jacobins*, x.

Further Reading

GILBERT, BIL. *God Gave Us This Country* (New York: Doubleday, 1990). Excellent study of Tecumseh in context of United States history in this period.

JOSEPHY, ALVIN, JR. "Tecumseh: The Greatest Indian," in *The Patriot Chiefs: A Chronicle of American Indian Resistance* (New York: Penguin Books, 1976). Good short biography.

KORNGOLD, RALPH. *Citizen Toussaint* (New York: Hill & Wang, 1965). Most readable biography.

OTT, THOMAS O. *The Haitian Revolution, 1789–1804* (Knoxville, TN: University of Tennessee Press, 1973). Best work on this subject.

George Sand and Harriet Beecher Stowe: Exploring "Woman's Sphere"

What did two popular nineteenth-century female authors see as the problems facing women? What did each see as the best sort of equality for women in their day? What impact did each have on her society?

In the famous American antislavery novel *Uncle Tom's Cabin*, author Harriet Beecher Stowe (1811–1896) has the slave Eliza, one of her main characters, dress in boy's clothing so she can cross Lake Erie with her husband and find freedom in Canada.[1] About the same time as this novel was written, a French author, Aurore Dudevant (1804–1876), adopted occasional use of men's clothing and a male pseudonym, George Sand, in order to achieve greater freedom as a person and writer.

The fact that both of these female writers and reformers saw that appearing male gave women greater freedom only hints at the difficulties facing creative women in the nineteenth century. Such women lived complex lives and faced serious legal and emotional problems.

If we look at industrializing nations like the United States and France a century and a half ago, we find patriarchal societies where most political, social, and economic rights were reserved to males. Unlike some feminist leaders today, few women then claimed equality based on their similarity to men. Rather, as the lives and careers of George Sand and Harriet Beecher Stowe illustrate, women unhappy with their situation argued for greater equality on the grounds that they were *different* from men.

"It will be in the female heart . . . as it always has been, that love and devotion, patience and pity, will find their true home. On woman falls the duty, in a world of brute passions, of preserving the virtues of charity and the Christian spirit." This statement may strike you as arrogant, sentimental, wrong-headed, or even correct. What is interesting is that these words on the character of women were written, not by the profoundly religious Harriet Beecher Stowe, but by George Sand, the scandalous Frenchwoman who took so many lovers that she was once called "the most obscene of women."[2]

Yet Stowe would have fully agreed with Sand's statement for, despite their quite different lifestyles, these two writers had much in common. Their lives spanned turbulent years of social and civil strife in France and the United States. And each woman played an active public role, Sand by writing revolutionary articles in Paris in 1848 and Stowe with her dramatic, history-making *Uncle Tom's Cabin*, published in 1852.

In their novels both writers addressed controversial social issues, although Sand generally focused on the injustices facing women and the lower classes in France, while Stowe became famous for describing the plight of slaves in the American south. Neither would qualify as a modern feminist, but each advocated the value of a woman's way of looking at things, and each felt that society could be improved if men understood and valued this viewpoint as well. Each wanted to see women gain substantial control over their personal lives and property. It was Sand, however, who engaged in serial monogamy [living with many men but only one at a time], who made this point much more directly than did the more traditional Stowe. Each woman believed that virtues taught at home, often called "woman's sphere" in the United States, were the foundation of civilization, though Stowe made this point far more powerfully than did Sand. By examining the lives and works of these authors, we can better understand both the difficulties facing women in the nineteenth century and debates over the role of women in our own time.

George Sand was born Amandine Aurore Lucie Dupin. Her father, an officer in Napoleon's army, traced his ancestry back to a king of Poland while her mother, Sophie Delaborde, was a dancer and the daughter of a Parisian bird seller. In later life after Aurore had taken the name George Sand as a way of earning respect in a profession dominated by males, she would make much of her working class background: "I was born . . . and started life in poverty, in the harsh, vagabond life of military camps. . . . I never forget that the blood of the [common] people ran in my veins."[3]

From her father's death in 1808, when Aurore was only four, until she married in 1822, her life was an emotional tug-of-war between her unstable mother and her paternal grandmother, Madame Dupin de Francueil. Since Sophie could not afford to support her daughter and therefore left her at Madame Dupin's estate at Nohant in return for financial support from her mother-in-law, the young Aurore felt abandoned. A cultured musician, Mme. Dupin de Francueil gave Aurore a good education and tried to train her in the ways of the aristocracy to better inoculate her against her "low-born" mother. However, the sensitive Aurore continued to crave her mother's love. When Aurore was nine, Sophie foolishly promised her that she would "rescue" her from the discipline of her grandmother and take her to Orleans where they would open a hat shop to support themselves. Aurore was crushed when her mother failed to follow through on this promise, and her grandmother made her feel worse by cruelly telling her that her mother's early sexual indiscretions made her "a lost woman."[4] Sand later recalled feeling that her parents had left her "a poor waif marked out for slavery, injustice, tedium, and eternal unrequited longing."[5] Beginning at age thirteen, she spent several years in a convent school in Paris where she had a mystical "conversion experience" which left her with the feeling that God could (and would) communicate directly with her, something Harriet Beecher Stowe also believed about herself. What one biographer has called Sand's "desperate search for parental affection" may account for her religious experience. This desire for acceptance would haunt George Sand the rest of her life; it helps explain the way she lived, and it gave great power to her fiction.[6]

At age eighteen, Aurore entered what proved to be an unhappy marriage with Baron Casimir Dudevant. Although they soon had a child, Maurice (named for Aurore's father), Casimir rejected Aurore's attempts to "improve" his mind, to get him to spend less time drinking and hunting and more time reading. Within three years, Aurore had formed a platonic [nonsexual] relationship with a "witty, elegant" young lawyer named Aurélien de Sèze. Although she tried to work out an agreement which would allow her to stay married to Casimir while continuing to visit and receive letters from Aurélien, by 1828 her marriage was clearly "on the rocks." In

September of that year, Aurore had a daughter, Solange, fathered by a young friend in Paris, Stéphane Ajasson. While Madame Dudevant was giving birth to Solange, she could hear Casimir in another room making love to a female servant.[7] In 1831, she moved to Paris, initially leaving the children with Casimir. Although not legally separated from Casimir until 1836, she immediately began living with a series of younger men, most of them artists. Jules Sandeau was the first, and it was his name which she took for her masculine pseudonym when she published her first novel, *Indiana*, in 1832. A succession of men—the composer Frédéric Chopin being the most famous—would follow in the coming years.

Indiana, as other Sand novels, was partly autobiographical. The heroine, Indiana, like Sand, is a young woman unhappily married to an older man, the jealous Colonel Delmare. During the course of this very "romantic" tale, Indiana falls in love with Raymon de Ramiére, an insincere nobleman who loves neither her nor her servant, Noun, whom he drove to suicide by refusing to marry her after getting her pregnant. After Indiana's husband discovers her affair with Raymon and beats her, she is saved from both Raymon and Colonel Delmare by her cousin Ralph, who takes her to a remote desert island where—after a failed mutual suicide attempt—they live out their days in seclusion.[8]

This first novel tells us much about how Sand viewed women's roles and rights. Clearly, the novel portrays women as the victim of both suppressed passions and legal injustice. Indiana, to Sand, "is love dashing her head blindly against all the obstacles of civilization." In a preface to the 1842 edition, Sand, aware that French laws gave women few rights, said she felt "that the laws which govern woman's existence in wedlock, in the family and in society are unjust and barbarous." She appeals to public opinion to change them, adding that she is not advocating revolution but only trying to "reconcile the welfare and the dignity of oppressed individuals . . . without modifying society itself." In the novel, Sand satirizes Colonel Delmare (modeled after her husband Casimir) as an "honest man" who does not steal from his neighbors or "ravish maidens in the public road" but who "may beat his wife, maltreat his servants, ruin his children and it is nobody's business" since "society punishes only those acts which are injurious to it; private life is beyond its jurisdiction." Later Indiana attacks Raymon's patriarchal notion of God:

Yours is the God of men, the king, the founder and upholder of your race; mine is the God of the universe, the creator, the preserver and the hope of all creatures. Yours made everything for you alone; mine made all created things for one another. . . . You think that God . . . authorizes you to possess the empire of the earth; . . . . the day will come when His breath will scatter you like grains of sand. . . . All your morality, all your principles, are simply the interests of your social class which you have raised to the dignity of laws. . . . it ill becomes you to invoke His name to crush . . . a poor, weak woman, to stifle the lamentations of a broken heart."[9]

But *Indiana* shows us more than Sand's conviction that neither women's passions nor their legal rights are taken seriously by her society; it also reveals Sand's romantic idealism, her search for an impossibly perfect love and lover. At one point in the novel, Indiana is "terrified" by her awareness "that she was of so little account in his [Raymon's] life while he was everything in hers." She wonders "in dismay if this man, for whom life had so many different aspects . . . could devote his whole mind to her, sacrifice all his ambitions to her."[10] In a later novel, *Lélia*, Sand's main character becomes emotionally and physically impotent because she intellectualizes love, calling it "the aspiration of our most ethereal part for the unknown." Her sister, a prostitute, tells her: "You should have applied your superior intellect to enjoy, not to deny, because if you don't, what good is intelligence?"[11]

Sand's biographers highlight her tendency to take as lovers younger men who were sensitive but frail artists, often afflicted with consumption [tuberculosis]. They suggest she selected men she could nurse and mother. Perhaps this was her way of compensating for her weak relationship with her own parents. One biographer found Sand "a man in her insistence on freedom, but a woman, too, craving the shelter of a 'home' with her children about her" and with "a passion for tending the sick."[12]

If Sand's childhood and early adult experiences drove her to be motherly and inhibited stable long-term relationships with men, they also made her more tolerant of the poor and of women trapped in unhappy marriages. Many of her sixty novels and hundreds of essays and articles deal with the plight of the poor. Her novel *Horace*, for example, contrasts the middle-class life of a flighty law student with that of a hard-working artisan. In the late 1830s and through the 1840s, she was attracted to the ideas of Pierre Leroux, who invented the word "socialism" (socialisme) and who felt that poverty was un-Christian and led people to a life of vice.[13] Her defense of women's rights, then, was not only an outgrowth of her own experience with Casimir; it was also set in this broader social-political context. In her second novel, *Valentine*, the heroine is a "naturally amiable and sweet" aristocrat who is in love with a peasant (Benedict) but forced to marry an insensitive nobleman who cares only about money. Sand's belief that people are born good but corrupted by society is expressed in her judgment that marriage between Valentine and Benedict was impossible because they came from different social classes: "Society stood between them and made their mutual choice absurd. . . . Providence created the admirable order of nature, men have destroyed it; whose is the fault?" At the end of the novel, Valentine and Benedict die in tragic events similar to those which befell Romeo and Juliet in Shakespeare's play.[14]

As Sand grew older, she turned from the writing of novels with a romantic or social message to those with more pastoral themes, exalting the simplicity of peasant life in her beloved province of Berry. Yet during the Revolution of 1848 she took time to defend the workers and promote her vague ideas of "socialism"—meaning for her little more than social and economic equality for the poor and a dislike for the lazy arrogance of the rich who "are not used to working."[15] Her sympathy for the lower classes of France was honored in 1870 when, during the Franco-Prussian War, one of the balloons used to help French leaders escape from the besieged city of Paris was named the *George Sand*.

It is interesting that despite her radical lifestyle and the many antimale statements in her works, Sand specifically opposed political rights, even suffrage, for women. She said that women needed civil equality in marriage and "equality before God," but, in the words of Sand's chief biographer, she "had . . . too low an opinion of the political intelligence of most members of her sex to be a suffragette." Besides, involvement in politics would undermine confidence in women's role as mothers: "How could even honest judges," she wrote:

> have confidence in women who, coming forward to claim the dignity now refused them in the family home, especially the sacred

authority over children which they are denied, demand . . . not peace in the household or freedom for their motherly affections, but the right to take part in the political struggle, a sword and a helmet, the right to condemn to death?[16]

Statements like this, stressing the importance of social rather than political equality for women, show Sand to be more politically conservative than her American counterpart, Harriet Beecher Stowe, who favored women's suffrage as a way to advance those special virtues of domesticity ("peace in the household . . . freedom for motherly affections") which both she and Sand thought important.

Yet, despite her advocacy of women's suffrage, Stowe was fundamentally a conservative person who ironically helped bring about a radical change—the end of slavery in the United States. Her emphasis on home as the appropriate sphere for female activity was an idea which both aided and restricted women in nineteenth-century America. On the one hand, it made women powerful judges of all issues related to home and family, especially the education and religious upbringing of children. Women could govern the domestic sphere without male interference; in exchange, however, the world beyond the home—the world of business, industry, and government—belonged solely to men.

The genius of Stowe's famous *Uncle Tom's Cabin*, then, was that it asked northern readers to end slavery, not because it was a political evil, but because of the devastating effect slavery had on the Christian family. Slavery was, in effect, a threat to "woman's sphere." This conviction and Stowe's sense of missionary idealism developed out of her childhood experiences, which were as challenging as those of George Sand, but very different. Harriet Beecher was the daughter of one of America's most famous Calvinist clergymen, Lyman Beecher. If George Sand had roots in the French aristocracy, Harriet Beecher was a member of the New England "nobility." The first Beechers arrived in New Haven, Connecticut, in 1638, just eighteen years after the *Mayflower*, and the family had remained important since that time. Lyman Beecher was such a powerful evangelical preacher and patriarch that all four of his sons became ministers and two of his three daughters—Catharine and Harriet—turned their religious zeal in the direction of social reform. Harriet would, in fact, "outpreach her father and all her gifted brothers combined"; if *Uncle Tom's Cabin* was a sermon (and it was), she would "count into her flock the peoples of the earth."[17]

But "Hattie" Beecher's religious vision would be notably different from that of her father, who believed in predestination [the belief that God has selected some people, before their birth, to be saved and others to be damned]. Especially after the death of her mother when she was four, Stowe tried hard to please her father, a difficult task since he could be a fiery preacher and strict disciplinarian one minute and a man in the depths of emotional despair and hypochondria [imaginary ill health] the next.

As a child, Stowe was convinced of her depravity. She did not escape this religious depression until her late teens, when she decided to believe in a compassionate Christ instead of the judgmental, monarchical Old Testament God of her father. Her decision would help change American history for, without it, *Uncle Tom's Cabin* would never have been written. Historian Ann Douglas argues that Harriet's personal decision was part of a much greater change she helped inspire in American religious history during the mid-nineteenth century. She kept the revivalistic spirit and moral tone of traditional Calvinism but softened or "feminized" its message in her novels by emphasizing the power of love over judgment. Her approach to Christianity also stressed the equality of all people in the eyes of God, relied on spreading the gospel through action (especially informal "peer counseling" among women) instead of preaching, and looked for God in everyday experience rather than in the thunderings of authority figures. Because of this, the type of Christianity found in Harriet Beecher Stowe's novels was an "explicit challenge [to] the male clerical establishment."[18]

It would be many years, however, before Stowe's fictional "ministry of the word" would begin in earnest. When her father took a position as director of the Lane Theological Seminary in Cincinnati in 1832, she and her sister Catharine moved to this western frontier town where Harriet married Calvin Stowe, a Lane professor. Between her wedding in 1836 (which she told her best friend she was "dreading" as an "overwhelming crisis") and the birth of her last child in Maine in 1850, she wrote only a few short stories and magazine pieces. She was devoted to her family and believed (as most of the female characters in her novels would later) that the well-regulated home was one of woman's greatest contributions to the world.

Yet, like Sand, she was not able to be only a housewife. In one letter, she told her friend Mary Dutton that she earned enough money from her "sketches" that she could now hire an extra servant and have more time to write. Later she accepted Calvin's insistence that she "must be a literary woman" and then asked him for "a room to myself, if I am to write." There was an undercurrent of half-suppressed discontent in comments she wrote during this period. In an 1845 letter she complained: "I am sick of the smell of sour milk, and sour meat, and sour everything, and then the clothes will not dry. . . . When the brain gives out . . . and one cannot think or remember anything, then what is to be done?" Other letters reveal some marital tensions; she and Calvin spent five of the first fifteen years of their married life apart—each in turn taking "rest cures" in Vermont. Calvin apparently had "intense and unremitting" sexual needs and, like Harriet's father, suffered from what she called "hypochondriac morbid instability."[19] One biographer claims that difficulties Stowe faced in her married life contributed to her passionate first novel.[20] Whether or not this was true, Stowe had learned to appreciate the sufferings of women and mothers. *Uncle Tom's Cabin* was her first and most powerful statement of her belief in the importance of the "woman's sphere."

When President Abraham Lincoln met Mrs. Stowe in the fall of 1862 and greeted her with the comment: "So this is the little lady who made this big war," he was referring not only to her size but also to the impact of *Uncle Tom's Cabin,* a book which sold 300,000 copies the year it was published (1852) and over half a million copies during the next five years. This work has been called "the most powerful and influential book of the nineteenth century" and "one of the most famous novels ever written."[21]

What made *Uncle Tom's Cabin* so popular and powerful was the way it personalized—even feminized—the issue of slavery, stressing that this institution tore mothers from their children in a manner that was both inhuman and, more importantly, un-Christian. In literary terms, *Uncle Tom's Cabin* may have been too sentimental (though the public liked sentimental novels), but it was "a great revival sermon, aimed directly at the conversion of its hearers."[22]

Tom, the novel's main character, lives successively with three masters. The first, kind Mr. Shelby in Kentucky, is forced to sell Tom because of hard times. Tom's second master, Augustine St. Clare, has mixed feelings about slavery and decides to free Tom, but fails to do so before he is unexpectedly killed. The infamous Simon Legree, Tom's last master, is a slaveowner so wicked that he even refuses to let his slaves sing religious hymns. He beats Tom fatally after Tom refuses to tell Legree the whereabouts of two slaves planning to escape. Other famous characters include Eliza (also sold by Shelby), who makes a daring escape with her son across the Ohio River by jumping from one ice floe to the next, and her husband, George, who is finally able to lead his family to freedom in Canada.

While sharing the journeys of these characters, we meet others whose actions reinforce the negative effect of slavery on Christian family life. There is Senator Bird of Ohio, who voted for the 1850 Fugitive Slave Law that required northerners to return runaway slaves to their owners; yet when Eliza shows up at his door and his wife admonishes him to put the Biblical injunction to "feed the hungry, clothe the naked, and comfort the desolate" ahead of politics, he provides help.[23] It was significant that Mary Bird, like Harriet herself, had recently lost a son the same age as Eliza's boy Harry. Mothers, Stowe was saying, understand other mothers.[24] Elsewhere in the novel, a slave mother drowns herself in the Ohio after discovering that her baby has been sold away from her during the night, and the Louisiana slave Cassy kills her newborn with opium after having two older children sold away from her. Ophelia, Augustine St. Clare's Vermont cousin, helps him care for his invalid wife and angelic child, Eva. Ophelia represents the virtues of a neat, well-organized kitchen (also found in the Quaker settlement where the Birds take Eliza).[25]

One of the criticisms made of Stowe's novel is its lack of subtlety; this is also the reason for its appeal. Uncle Tom and Eva St. Clare are exaggerated Christ figures. Tom helps St. Clare find faith and then dies to save others; Eva, as she nears death, asks her father to free Tom and reminds him: "Papa, these poor creatures love their children as much as you do me." And, just in case anyone missed the point, Stowe ends her novel with an appeal to northern mothers to end slavery:

> Mothers of America,—you who have learned, by the cradles of your own children, to love and feel for all mankind. . . . I beseech you, pity those mothers that are constantly made childless by the American slave trade! . . . The people of the free states . . . are more guilty for it, before God, than the South, in that they have not the apology of education or custom.[26]

Aside from Tom himself, the strongest characters in *Uncle Tom's Cabin* tend to be female. Some are white women like Mrs. Shelby, Mrs. Bird, and Ophelia who deplore the evils of slavery and the domestic disorder it brings but leave the final decisions to men. Eva represents women of strong character who seek the reward for their suffering in heaven, while black slave women like Eliza and Cassy have the strength to rebel and escape to a better life in Canada.

Uncle Tom's Cabin appealed to many not only because it was a powerful, sentimental novel but also because it was as much about the role of women in American society as it was about slavery. Two years after *Uncle Tom's Cabin* was published, Stowe wrote an "Appeal to the Women of the Free States," urging them to petition Congress to prevent the extension of slavery. Her language is powerful and direct: "However ambition and love of political power may blind the stronger sex, God has given to woman a deeper and more immovable knowledge, in those holier feelings, which are peculiar to womanhood, and which guard the sacredness of the family." By seeing slavery as a threat to the sanctity of "woman's sphere" Stowe, says one critic, "designates slavery as a domestic issue for American women to adjudicate and manage. . . . abolishing slavery means . . . erasing [a] reminder of the precariousness of the feminine sphere."[27]

For Stowe and other nineteenth-century American female reformers, especially in the post-Civil War generation, the virtues found in the "feminine sphere" of the home stood in opposition to the spirit of greedy capitalism which dominated the world of business in this "Gilded Age." "Our men are sufficiently money-making," Sarah Josepha Hale wrote in the *Ladies Magazine*. "Let us keep our women and children from the contagion as long as possible."[28] In Stowe's later "social novels," *Pink and White Tyranny, My Wife and I* (both 1871), and *We and Our Neighbors* (1873), she addresses more explicitly the question of women's roles. Here Stowe's male characters are in charge of business while "the woman and her educated daughters [are] in charge of Culture." Stowe believed women had the right to own property, and the right to work and be paid equal to men, all things George Sand would have applauded. But the case for women's rights, she argued, rested on women's moral superiority. Women's votes, for example, "would close grogshops [taverns], . . . stop the traffic in spirits" and improve society, as women were already working to improve the family.[29]

Stowe wanted a world in which woman's work would be recognized as equally important as that of men. Like George Sand, she did not want to challenge the fundamental patriarchal structure of society. In fact, in *My Wife and I* she pointedly attacked the radical feminists of her day, such as Victoria Woodhull, satirizing them in the person of a loose-living character named Audacia Dangyereyes, whom she calls an advocate of "the wildest principles of modern French communism." By modern feminist standards, of course, keeping women in the home—even as domestic dictators—was a good way to thwart equality for women and preserve the patriarchal society. Less than a century later, Betty Friedan's *Feminine Mystique* would find oppressive the very "domesticity" which Stowe extolled.[30]

George Sand and Harriet Beecher Stowe never met. After *Uncle Tom's Cabin* was published in France, Sand offered Mrs. Stowe the following backhanded compliment: "I cannot say she has talent as one understands it in the world of letters, but she has . . . the genius of goodness, not that of a man of letters, but of the saint." When Stowe went to Europe in 1853 and visited Paris, she wanted to meet Sand's but was told that her reputation would suffer if she did so.[31] Had they met, perhaps they would have found more in common than either might have thought.

Both women had a stronger spirit of independence than most of their contemporaries, either male or female. Both were determined to be writers and each wanted her writing to make a difference. Both succeeded admirably, though they shared an exaggerated belief in the ability of a woman's love and virtue to change the world. Sand's fiction is attractive to feminists today because it conveys the anguish which this sensitive woman felt as she struggled to find her ideal lover. Sand is also better than Stowe at identifying problems facing women; Stowe—despite the ultimate failure of her "domesticity" strategy—is better at suggesting solutions. Yet they both *did* change the world. Sand was one of the first modern women to not only demand sexual equality with men but live as if she had it. Her novels are still read by those interested in how women *felt* about life in the mid-nineteenth century. Harriet Beecher Stowe's *Uncle Tom's Cabin* did contribute to the coming of the American Civil War. Lincoln was right, at least in part.

Did either contribute significantly to women's equality? Here the jury is still out—evaluations of their contributions to modern feminism are mixed. Neither would be troubled by this, for each lived life to a fuller extent than generally thought possible in her day. And although both would have specific disagreements with modern women's rights activists, their aim—to speak as women and be heard—would be shared by these writers and their late twentieth-century "sisters."

Notes

1. Harriet Beecher Stowe, *Uncle Tom's Cabin* (New York: Bantam Books, 1981; original 1851–1852), 381–382; Stowe also used the male pseudonym "Franklin" when writing an antislavery letter to a Cincinnati newspaper in 1836—see Forrest Wilson, *Crusader in Crinoline: The Life of Harriet Beecher Stowe* (Westport, CT: Greenwood Press, 1972; original, 1941), 179.
2. Andre Maurois, *Lelia: The Life of George Sand*, trans. by Gerard Hopkins (New York: Harper and Brothers, 1954), 324; J. M. Quadrado, "To George Sand: A Refutation," in *George Sand: Winter in Majorca* (Chicago: Academy Press, Ltd., 1978), 200.
3. From a letter to Charles Poncy (December 1843), in *George Sand in Her Own Words*, trans. and edited by Joseph Barry (Garden City, NY: Doubleday Anchor, 1979), 287–288.
4. Curtis Cate, *George Sand: A Biography* (Boston: Houghton Mifflin, 1975), 35–39, 52–54.
5. George Sand, *My Life*, trans. and adapted by Dan Hofstadter (New York: Harper and Row, 1979), 123.
6. Cate, *Sand*, 62–66; Sand, *My Life*, 145–150; Maurois, *Lelia*, 324; Renee Winegarten, *The Double Life of George Sand: Woman and Writer* (New York: Basic Books, 1978), 33–34.
7. Samuel Edwards, *George Sand* (New York: David McKay Co., 1972), 50; see also Cate, *Sand*, 112–126.
8. See George Sand, *Indiana*, trans. by George Burnham Ives (Chicago: Academy Press Ltd., 1978).
9. Sand, *Indiana*, xxiv, xxviii, xxxii, 96, 224.
10. *Ibid.*, 115.
11. George Sand, *Lelia*, trans. by Maria Espinosa (Bloomington: Indiana University Press, 1978; original, 1833), 36, 106.
12. See Maurois, *Lelia*, 92, 140; see also 103, 140, 173, 261; Cate, *Sand*, 321–322; Winegarten, *Double Life*, 186–187; Joseph Barry, *Infamous Woman: The Life of George Sand* (Garden City, NY: Doubleday, 1976), 34–35, 67–68, 73.
13. See Cate, *Sand*, 493–497.
14. George Sand, *Valentine*, trans. by George Burnham Ives (Chicago: Cassandra Editions, 1978; original 1832), see especially 108–113, 137, 326–333.

15. Sand, *In Her Own Words*, 355–390.

16. Cate, *Sand*, xxx–xxxi; Sand, *In Her Own Words*, 404–405; see also 411–413. For some of Sand's strongest antimale statements, see 339–340 of this work.

17. Wilson, *Crusader*, 21.

18. Ann Douglas, *The Feminization of American Culture* (Garden City, NY: Doubleday, 1988; original, 1977), 4–12, 244–256; Joan D. Hedrick, "'Peaceable Fruits': The Ministry of Harriet Beecher Stowe," *American Quarterly* (September 1988), 308; see also Dorothy Berkson, "Millennial Politics and the Feminine Fiction of Harriet Beecher Stowe," in Elizabeth Ammons, *Critical Essays on Harriet Beecher Stowe* (Boston: G. K. Hall, 1980), 246–249.

19. Mary Kelley, "Harriet Beecher Stowe: 'Changing to Nobody Knows Who,'" in Jeanne Boydston, Mary Kelley, Anne Margolis, *The Limits of Sisterhood: The Beecher Sisters on Women's Rights and Woman's Sphere* (Chapel Hill: University of North Carolina Press, 1988), 52, 62, 67–70, 73; Mary Kelley, "At War With Herself: Harriet Beecher Stowe as Woman in Conflict Within the Home," *American Studies*, Volume 19 (1978), 31.

20. John R. Adams, *Harriet Beecher Stowe* (New York: Twayne Publishers, 1963), 19, 27.

21. Wilson, *Crusader*, 484; Robert F. Lucid, "Harriet Beecher Stowe," *McGraw-Hill Encyclopedia of World Biography* (New York: McGraw-Hill, 1973), 240; Winifred E. Wise, *Harriet Beecher Stowe: Woman With a Cause* (New York: G. P. Putnam's Sons, 1965), 10, 165.

22. Douglas, *Feminization*, 244.

23. Stowe, *Uncle Tom's Cabin*, 77.

24. In a letter to the abolitionist Eliza Cabot Follen (December 1852), Stowe wrote that it was at her son's deathbed and grave in 1849 "that I learned what a poor slave mother may feel when her child is torn away from her." After *Uncle Tom's Cabin* was finished (it began as a short story), Harriet said on several occasions that "The Lord Himself wrote it. I was but an instrument in His hand." Whether or not *Uncle Tom's Cabin* was so "inspired," the story clearly conveyed the personal passion which she felt on this subject (see Wilson, *Crusader*, 270ff.).

25. Stowe, *Uncle Tom's Cabin*, 129, 131, 154ff., 365.

26. Stowe, *Ibid.*, 301, 276, 441.

27. Boydston et. al., *Limits of Sisterhood*, 180–181; Gillian Brown, "Getting in the Kitchen with Dinah: Domestic Politics in *Uncle Tom's Cabin*," *American Quarterly*, Volume 36 (Fall 1984), 506. It is interesting that none of the blacks in *Uncle Tom's Cabin* are weak, despite later use of the term "Uncle Tom" by modern blacks to describe someone who is too passive and accepting of white leadership. See Beatrice A. Anderson, "Uncle

Tom: A Hero at Last," *American Transcendental Quarterly* (June 1991), 95–108.27.
28. Quoted in Brown, "Getting in the Kitchen with Dinah," 505.
29. Alice C. Crozier, *The Novels of Harriet Beecher Stowe* (New York: Oxford, 1969), 157; Stowe, "The Woman Question," *Atlantic Monthly* (December 1865), 672–683, quoted in Boydston et. al., *Limits of Sisterhood*, 266–269.
30. Harriet Beecher Stowe, *My Wife and I* (Boston: Houghton Mifflin, 1896; original, 1871), 268–283; Douglas, *Feminization*, 11–12. See Betty Friedan, *The Feminine Mystique* (New York: W. W. Norton, 1963).
31. Cate, *Sand*, 329, 429–430.

Further Reading

CATE, CURTIS. *George Sand: A Biography* (Boston: Houghton Mifflin, 1975). Comprehensive, readable, and fair presentation of life of Sand.

SAND, GEORGE. *George Sand in Her Own Words*, trans. and edited by Joseph Barry (Garden City, NY: Doubleday Anchor, 1979). Good sampling of her fiction and essays; contains lengthy portions of early novels.

STOWE, HARRIET BEECHER. *Uncle Tom's Cabin*. Many editions. A must reading for understanding of Stowe, slavery, and "domesticity" in the 1850s.

WILSON, FORREST. *Crusader in Crinoline: The Life of Harriet Beecher Stowe* (Westport, CT: Greenwood Press, 1972; original, 1941). Old but comprehensive biography which should be supplemented with some recent periodical literature and some of the newer specialized studies.

CHAPTER 7

Bismarck and Ito: Conservatives and Constitutions

How can a constitution be written to make a nation look democratic while it is in fact still controlled by conservative aristocrats? What are some consequences of such a "premodern" constitution?

Modern political constitutions are, for most of us, necessary but dull documents. Following the example of the ones drawn up by the United States or by the French revolutionaries some two hundred years ago, these documents usually list the rights of citizens and spell out the powers of government. While such documents are not exactly bedtime reading, they are important in the process of modern nation building. Constitutions presuppose but also help build a consensus about what the people in a particular state consider important; they also help people distinguish themselves from their neighbors. Perhaps most important, such documents give most groups in the state a sense of security. By offering some civil and political rights (usually), they give the masses a feeling of participation and a sense of belonging. By defining the rights and limits of government, they reassure people in business and help promote economic development. They even aid rulers by giving them the comfort of knowing that the people have agreed, by adopting or accepting the constitution, not to overthrow the existing government—unless absolutely necessary.

The nineteenth century was a time when being modern meant having a constitution, when the terms "nationalism" and "constitutionalism" were almost synonymous. The most important nation-state created in nineteenth-century Europe was the German empire, founded in 1871 after three wars presided over by the Prussian chancellor Otto von Bismarck (1815–1898). Certainly the most dynamic nation-state in eastern Asia during the past century has been Japan. Japan began the process of nation building in 1868 with the Meiji Restoration, but its constitution was not promulgated [presented to the people] until 1889. This document, adapted from Bismarck's Prussian constitution, was largely the work of Ito Hirobumi (1841–1909).

Today, the very words "Germany" and "Japan" tend to evoke similar associations for Americans. We think immediately of economic competition and World War II. The parallels a century ago were equally striking. Bismarck's Prussia, the largest state in north Germany, had a reputation for military strength until it was humiliated by the armies of the French emperor Napoleon in 1806. Ito was thirteen in 1853 when Commodore Matthew Perry arrived in Japan to demand political and economic privileges for the Americans. He could do this because the Western nations possessed superior weapons and advanced industrial technology. Their desire to compete on equal terms in the world drove both Bismarck and Ito to create strong, centralized nation-states. Both realized that new political structures were necessary before this could happen. Each wanted to preserve as much conservative political power as possible while adopting only as much political modernization as was necessary to create a strong nation-state. Although each succeeded in maintaining the power of the ruling class, neither man was able to limit the growth of popular antigovernment parties as much as he had hoped. Both tried to limit popular sovereignty [rule by the people]. Both left a flawed nation as a legacy to later leaders. The wars fought by Germany and Japan in the past century were, in part, a consequence of the way constitutions were written and nationalism used in these countries in the late nineteenth century.

Otto von Bismarck's life and career was marked by a tension between his conservative political goals and the sometimes radical methods he used to pursue them. This tension was foreshadowed in his parentage. His father was a Prussian nobleman, a "Junker," [pronounced "yoongker"] whose family had owned land in Brandenburg for five centuries. His mother (with no "von" before her name to indicate nobility) was simply Wilhelmine Mencken, a middle-class descendant of civil servants and academicians. From his father, Bismarck learned to love the land and respect the values of the agricultural classes. From his more cosmopolitan and ambitious mother, Bismarck acquired cleverness, sophistication, and an urban education not common among his Junker neighbors. Some historians believe that Bismarck's attempt to imitate both of his very different parents made him a neurotic genius.[1]

Genius or not, Bismarck's early years were unproductive. His student years at the University of Göttingen were marred by his love of drinking, passionate love affairs, and delight in duels (he fought twenty-five duels and suffered only one wound). His less than brilliant university career ended in Berlin, where he crammed to pass his law exam in 1834–1835. Bismarck's aggressive tendencies were diminished somewhat by a religious experience in 1846 and by his marriage to Johanna von Puttkamer in 1847. Yet the "natural lust for combat" that led Bismarck to duel appeared later in struggles against political opponents and foreign rulers. Sometimes he expressed it more directly. In 1866, after Bismarck had become Prussian chancellor, a would-be assassin fired upon him five times on a Berlin street. As the man finished firing, the tall Junker turned upon him and seized him by the throat.[2]

Although he spent the seven years before his wedding managing his family's estates, Bismarck's real love was diplomacy and statecraft. He was able to pursue this after his king appointed him Prussian representative to the Diet of the German Confederation at Frankfurt in May 1851. During the 1850s the Prussians and Austrians were struggling for control of the other German states after a group of middle-class revolutionaries had failed to unify Germany in 1848. In his role as Prussian ambassador to the Diet [where representatives from each German state met periodically to discuss common problems], Bismarck tried to promote Prussian domination of a new German national state which would exclude Austria. The Austrian empire at this time was ruled by Germans but included many non-German peoples living in southeastern Europe. During this decade Bismarck also pursued his goal of Prussian leadership in Germany when he served for a time as the Prussian ambassador to Russia.

Bismarck's chief advantage was that he knew precisely what he wanted: He favored not only Prussian domination of Germany but also a Prussia in which the Junker nobility, and not the middle-class liberals or (worse yet) democrats and socialists, would dominate the government and the army. He got his chance to work directly to create such a state in the fall of 1862 when the Prussian king asked him to become chancellor [or prime minister] and help the monarch out of a constitutional conflict in which he had become embroiled.

King William and his war minister wanted to modernize the Prussian army by drafting more men and keeping them in active service for three years instead of two. They also wanted to do away with the reserve, or *Landwehr*, with its supposedly less professional middle-class officers. Since this reform would mean a fifty percent increase in the military budget and a twenty-five percent tax increase, the king was required to ask the Prussian Parliament, or Diet, to approve the expense. In order to maintain some middle-class influence over the military, the members of the Prussian Diet wanted to keep both the *Landwehr* and the two-year period of service. This would give the Junker officers less time to indoctrinate new conscripts. For two years, the king was unable to get the Diet to approve the army bill. By 1862 when Bismarck was made chancellor, the two sides were deadlocked.

Bismarck showed both determination and shrewdness in solving the king's problem. First he told the members of the Diet that the German people preferred a strong army and national unification to liberal constitutional limits on the power of the government. Then he proved he was right and called the bluff of the liberals by telling the Prussian bureaucrats to collect the taxes to pay for the army reform even though the Diet had not approved them. They did, and the people paid. Bismarck put the capstone on the liberal defeat in 1866. After the Seven Weeks' War in which the newly strengthened Prussian army decisively defeated Austria, Bismarck offered the Prussian Diet an Indemnity Bill. He would admit the government had been wrong in illegally collecting taxes if the Diet would retroactively approve the collection of those taxes. The bill passed 230 to 75. Forced to choose between liberal restraints on government and national power, the liberals chose power. Bismarck sensed they would.

After defeating Austria, Prussia was free to organize the North German Confederation, a union of all German states except Austria, Bavaria, Württemberg, and Baden, in 1867. In 1871, after a war with France which Bismarck helped provoke and which resulted in another quick Prussian victory, the south German states (except Austria) joined in creating the German empire. The Prussian king became Kaiser (Emperor) William I. Bismarck created the constitution for the new state, and this document shows how the "iron chancellor," as he was later known, was able to combine modern political forms with careful protection of traditional aristocratic values.

Perhaps the most modern feature of Bismarck's constitution was the election of the lower house of the legislature (Reichstag) by universal male suffrage. A man did not even have to own property in order to vote. Bismarck's fellow Prussian conservatives were shocked at such radicalism. However, the appearance of popular government was deceptive. In the first place, the Reichstag had little real governing power. Representatives could not introduce or "initiate" legislation, but could only discuss and vote on what was brought to them by the government. All members of the "executive branch" of the government were appointed by the emperor and did not have to "respond" to the Reichstag. That body could not vote "no-confidence" in the chancellor, or chief minister, and thus force a change in the government, as the British Parliament could do.

In the upper chamber of the legislature, the Federal Council or Bundesrat, conservative forces clearly dominated. Like the United States Senate, the Bundesrat had to approve all treaties and other legislation. However, members were not elected but appointed by the various state governments. They voted as instructed. Prussia, the largest state in the new empire, controlled three-fifths of the territory and seventeen of fifty-eight seats in the Bundesrat. Although the Reichstag did have to approve military spending, control of the army and the entire civil administration remained in the hands of the emperor. The entire constitution was seen as a *gift* from the princes to the German people rather than as a *right* of the people.[3] The federal constitution contained no bill of rights; civil liberties and social services were left to the individual states.

Bismarck's government was designed to be authoritarian with some democratic window dressing. Popular elections to the Reichstag would mobilize national sentiment and give people a feeling of participation in the government, while real power would remain in the hands of the aristocracy and upper-middle-class business interests. But it did not work out that way. First, to be a genuine national symbol, the Reichstag had to be used; besides, the government was required to seek approval for legislation, especially that which involved spending money. Second, from 1871 to 1890, when Bismarck was forced to resign, the growing working class electorate sent increasing numbers of socialist delegates to the Reichstag. Bismarck and the emperor refused to work with the socialists, whom they considered radical. This would eventually bring legislative business to a standstill. Third, the constitution did not work as designed. Although the emperor himself had absolute authority over both the army and the civil administration, including the appointment of the chancellor and final decision on Reichstag measures, in practice Emperor William I generally took advice from Bismarck, whose skillful manipulation of the various political constituencies was needed to keep the system working reasonably well. When William I's grandson, William II, took over in 1890, he wanted the constitution to work as it had been designed on paper, with himself in charge. Bismarck was dismissed, and William's attempts to use the constitution as written soon led to disaster.

As perhaps the most skillful politician of his century, Bismarck was able to maintain political equilibrium both at home and in Europe like a man standing at the center of a seesaw, applying weight as needed to keep his potential enemies in the air. During the 1870s, he allied himself with the liberals in the Reichstag to establish laws (such as those removing trade barriers among German states and setting up a common coinage) which would promote industrialization. During the 1880s, Bismarck allied himself with the Catholic Center Party (which he had attacked in the 1870s) and the conservatives while attacking the liberals and the socialists. This policy of unifying people by creating common enemies was also pursued in European diplomacy. Bismarck tied both Russia and Austria to Germany with alliances in which he promised to help either country if the other attacked. He also tied himself to Russia in the Reinsurance Treaty of 1887 in order to forestall any alliance between France and Russia which would encircle Germany. At the Berlin Conference in 1878, he prevented Russia from taking too much territory in the Balkans and thus disturbing the balance between Russia and Austria in that area. In 1885 at another Berlin Conference, he helped provide for a friendly division of European territory in Africa. Bismarck clearly wished to keep peace at home and abroad, yet he could do this only by a delicate balancing of forces which his successors were not able to continue. Their attempts to imitate him, in a world of changing economic and political conditions, degenerated into bluster and bullying. After 1890, Germany's alliances led to war instead of peace.

Over a decade after Bismarck's forced retirement in 1890 and just a few years before his own death, the Japanese statesman Ito Hirobumi wrote "Some Reminiscences of the Grant of the New Constitution." In this essay, Ito summarized the policy of the Japanese government in 1868 after the Meiji Restoration, a coup led by young aristocratic warrior-bureaucrats [samurai] from several of the major domains [large feudal estates]. These Meiji bureaucrats, or oligarchs, as they came to be known, abolished the Tokugawa Shogunate [a form of government in which a military leader or shogun ruled in the name of the emperor] and proclaimed the young emperor the power center of a new Japanese government. These men wished to modernize the country and were determined to meet the threat posed by the Western powers. In words which might have been used by a German statesman at the same time, the emperor, as Ito remembered, swore:

> to educate the people to the requirements of a constitutional state, to fortify the nation with the best results and resources of modern civilization, and thus to secure for the country prosperity, strength, and . . . the . . . recognized status of membership upon an equal footing in the family of the most powerful and civilized nations of the world.[4]

To seek a place in the sun, among the great powers, was as important to late-nineteenth-century Japanese as it was to their German counterparts. From 1868, when he was made an imperial councilor, to his death in 1909, Ito was a part of a process of modernization which sought to combine Western economic and military power with the social and political stability of traditional Japan. The results of this attempt, as in Germany, were mixed.

Ito hailed from the village of Tsukari in the domain of Choshu in southern Japan. His father, Hayashi Juzo, though a farmer, was descended from the samurai warrior class, the rough equivalent of medieval European knights, and traced his family back to the third son of Emperor Kiorei (290–214 BC).[5] Ito received the education of a samurai and grew up sharing this group's dislike for foreigners who demanded special commercial and legal rights such as extraterritoriality [being subject to their own laws rather than those of the country in which they resided]. Many Japanese warriors, especially those in the western domains of Choshu, Satysuma, Tosa, and Hizen, wished to overthrow the shogun because he had made deals with the foreigners. Leaders in the western domains wished to restore the power of the emperor—in whose name the shogun's family had ruled Japan for over two centuries—*and* fight to throw out the foreigners. By 1864, as a result of a unique journey, Ito would be one of the first young samurai to suggest restoring the emperor and making temporary peace with the foreigners as well.

In May 1863, Ito and four other young samurai secretly boarded a freighter to sneak to Shanghai and then England in order to learn Western seafaring techniques. Ito returned to Japan six months later with some knowledge of English and the conviction that Japan must become a modern nation. The way to do this was to learn from the foreigners rather than expel them. This was a more mature Ito than the young man who, several years earlier, had helped burn down the house of the British diplomatic representative in Yedo because it had been built on sacred ground.[6]

After the Meiji Restoration, Ito and his fellow oligarchs faced the task of building a modern nation-state in Japan. Their job was to create a truly central administration to replace the old domains. Japan also needed a national army, modern communications, a common currency, and national laws. The difficulty of this task of modernization is illustrated by the story of how peasants cut telegraph wires because they believed the wires would be used to transmit their blood to quench the thirst of the foreigners. Other, less fearful peasants decided that if the wires could carry thoughts, they ought to be able to carry packages. Riders had to be hired to keep the lines free and uncut.[7]

Ito and his colleagues proceeded slowly and carefully in devising a political system. It took them over twenty years to promulgate a constitution designed to strengthen the state and the allegiance of the people. Ito was sent on three missions abroad during his career, and the second of these in 1882–1883 took him to Bismarck's Germany, whose constitution the Japanese used as a model for their own. A Prussian, Carl Friedrich Hermann Roessler, was even a member of the five-man committee which wrote the Japanese document.[8] Ito himself shared the Prussian belief that a legislature dominated by political parties should not control the imperial government. When one of his colleagues proposed an English-style constitution with an executive responsible to a parliament, or diet, Ito strongly opposed him, writing:

> Your memorial calls for selecting the heads of ministries and imperial household officials from political parties. In the final analysis this is equivalent to transferring the imperial prerogatives to the people. Such heretical views should not be held by any subject.[9]

When finally written and presented as "a voluntary gift of the Emperor to his subjects," the Japanese constitution continued the broad powers of the emperor over the military and civil administration. Civil rights were guaranteed to the people "only within the limits of the law." The Japanese authors thought they had solved the problems of getting money for the budget from the lower house, or Diet. If the Diet could not agree on a budget, the budget from the previous year would automatically come into force. While a clever idea in theory, in practice the lower house attained control over the budget since the Japanese government, and especially the military, was expanding throughout the late nineteenth century and needed increases every year.[10]

During his long career, Ito served his emperor in many ways. He was the chief minister, or premier, on four separate occasions and at other times was minister for finance and "home affairs" and presiding officer of the House of Peers, or upper chamber of the legislature. At one point in the mid-1880s, Ito's positions as premier, head of the staff of the imperial household, and chairman of the commission to draw up the constitution gave him powers comparable to those of Bismarck.[11] When it became clear that political parties were going to remain a force in Japan, despite the dislike of the oligarchs for party government, Ito responded by organizing his own party in 1900. The Seiyukai, or [literally] "friends of the Constitution," Party won the Diet elections in 1900. Ito became premier again, and set a healthy example of working within the political process rather than just manipulating the existing parties as Bismarck had done. Ito spent the last years of his life attempting to moderate the influence of the military in foreign policy but was unable to avoid a war with Russia over Korea, which the Japanese won. In 1905 he became the first "resident general" for Japan in Korea and four years later was assassinated by a Korean nationalist. With Ito's moderating influence gone, and using his death as a pretext, the Japanese annexed the peninsula outright in 1910.

Increasing domination of Japanese politics by the military led to more wars, culminating in World War II. As in Germany, the civilians supported these wars as long as the army was successful. Also as in Germany, political parties increased their influence in the generation after Ito's death, despite the authoritarian system of government envisioned in the original constitution. Of course, in Japan loyalty to the semidivine emperor was a more important nation-building force than were popular elections to the Diet. This fact, as well as the more limited suffrage in Japan (only slightly more than one percent of the populace could vote in 1889), were important differences in the politics of the two new states. Another cultural difference between the two nations was the more dominant position of the male in Japanese society. Twenty-five years after his death, Ito's biographer wrote, with only a hint of apology, that his subject, "like all privileged men of his race, . . . made the rounds of the various inns where wine, women, and the noisy twang of the shamisen [musical instrument] served to conjure up that delectable freedom of oblivion for one brief night."[12] If Bismarck enjoyed such pleasures, the customs of his society required that he do so less publicly.

In neither of these two modern nations did the authoritarian groups lose their ability to shape the destiny of the country until the middle of the twentieth century. Ironically, Adolf Hitler did more to destroy the old Prussian Junker class than did Germany's enemies in World War II; Hitler was particularly upset when members of this group helped organize a plot to kill him in 1944. In Japan, while members of the old oligarchic families continued to influence national life in the years after World War II, the military clique had lost its power and the post-World War II constitution clearly announced "that sovereign power resides with the people."

We can say then that the attempts by Bismarck and Ito to combine the social and political values of an agrarian warrior aristocracy with the industrial and military power of a dynamic modern state had only limited success. In both cases, the new nation was flawed. On the one hand liberal capitalists wished to use government to create a new industrial society. A move in this direction would necessarily require giving some power to the working class, however much the industrialists resented doing so. On the other hand, the more conservative rulers distrusted both the upstart businessmen and industrialists and the working masses. These traditionalist rulers, however, did value the ability of the industrialists to make guns and the ability of the men of the lower classes to use them in war.

Perhaps the best example of the desire of these rulers to keep their power while pretending to share it was the constitutions which they devised. When a government issues a constitution, it is saying that people are governed by laws which will be fairly enforced. It is also saying that people have a right to know what the rules of government are. These points, of course, both the Prussian Junkers and the Japanese oligarchs would concede. But it is only a short step from having clear rules to saying that the people who have the right to these rules also have the right to change them. This is the principle of popular sovereignty—one which the conservative Bismarck and Ito would not accept but, in the final analysis, could not deny.

Notes

1. Theodore S. Hamerow, editor, *Otto von Bismarck: A Historical Assessment* (Boston: D.C. Heath, 1962), 13–14; see Otto Pflanze, "Toward a Psychoanalytic Interpretation of Bismarck," *American Historical Review* (April 1972), 419–444.
2. Otto Pflanze, *Bismarck and the Development of Germany. The Period of Unification, 1815–1871* (Princeton: Princeton University Press, 1963), 59.
3. Gordon A. Craig, *Germany, 1866–1945* (Oxford: Oxford University Press, 1978), 42–44.
4. Ito Hirobumi, "Some Reminiscences of the Grant of the New Constitution," in *Fifty Years of New Japan*, compiled by Count Shigenobu Okuma; English version edited by Marcus B. Huish, Volume I, Second Edition (London: Smith, Elder and Company, 1910), 125–126.
5. Kengi Hamada, *Prince Ito* (Tokyo: The Sanseido Company, Ltd., 1936), 5–6. East Asians typically place the surname last in English. Hirobumi's last name is Ito rather than Hayashi because his father, in financial difficulty, had himself adopted by a samurai, Ito Buhei. This practice was common in pre-Meiji Japan.
6. *Ibid.*, 34–40.
7. Hugh Borton, *Japan's Modern Century* (New York: Ronald Press, 1955), 69–71, 79, 173.
8. George Akita, *Foundations of Constitutional Government in Modern Japan, 1868–1900* (Cambridge, MA: Harvard University Press, 1967), 60–63.
9. *Ibid.*, 36–38.
10. Hamada, *Prince Ito*, 96; see Borton, *Japan's Modern Century*, 126, 145, and the entire constitution in Appendix IV, 490–507.
11. Borton, *Japan's Modern Century*, 137.
12. Hamada, *Prince Ito*, 211–212.

Further Reading

AKITA, GEORGE. *Foundations of Constitutional Government in Modern Japan, 1868–1900* (Cambridge, MA: Harvard University Press, 1967). Scholarly, clear account of the change of government.

HAMADA, KENGI. *Prince Ito* (Tokyo: The Sanseido Company, Ltd., 1936). Flowery but entertaining biography by an aristocrat. Notice the date and handle with care if you cannot read Japanese, since this is the only life in English.

HAMEROW, THEODORE S. Editor. *Otto von Bismarck: A Historical Assessment* (Boston: D. C. Heath, 1961, 1973). Many different opinions of his contribution to German and European history. A good place to start.

CHAPTER 8

Graves and Hemingway:
Reactions to War and Death

How did two Western writers cope, each in different ways, with the personal challenges posed by twentieth-century violence and warfare?

World War I (1914–1918) was a turning point in Western history. This was true not only because ten million men were killed or wounded on the various battlefields of Europe, Africa, and Asia, and not even because of the shocking way in which many of them died—running across open fields into barbed wire, gas, and machine-gun fire. Nor did massive dislocation of civilian populations or great political changes make the war so significant. Greater dislocations, political changes, and even higher casualty figures accompanied World War II.

The "Great War," as this conflict was called until a greater one came along twenty years later, was a turning point in modern history primarily because it sent a shock wave rippling through European politics, culture, and society. Europeans, used to dominating the rest of the world, were forced to realize that in the words of a French poet, "we too are mortal." European self-confidence was shaken. The most technologically advanced civilization in history could no longer take its survival, much less its superiority, for granted. Too much damage had been done to the physical landscape of Europe and to the emotions of Europeans by the four years of senseless slaughter.

Among the intellectuals who witnessed the change brought about by the war were two literary men, the English poet Robert Graves (1895–1985) and the American novelist Ernest Hemingway (1899–1961). Both men were seriously wounded during the war, yet both survived to pursue brilliant literary careers shaped subtly or overtly by their brush with death. The war affected the way they

89

perceived the postwar world. An age of innocence, optimism, and belief in individualism ended in the trenches of France in the years after 1914. It was replaced by a world in which death became both more routine and more mechanized. Graves expressed his dissatisfaction with both the old world and the new in his famous autobiography written in 1929, *Good-bye to All That*. In the same year, Hemingway published his classic novel set in World War I, *A Farewell to Arms*. These two men, in these works and others, defined two twentieth-century reactions to a world preoccupied with violence and death.

Robert Graves grew up in a world both privileged and innocent. He was born July 24, 1895, at Wimbledon, England. His father was an Irish poet and scholar who could trace his noble ancestors back four hundred years. Amalie von Ranke Graves, his mother, hailed from a German noble family; her uncle was the famous historian Leopold von Ranke. Robert had kind things to say about his father but described his mother as compulsive and overprotective. She brought up her children, he wrote, "to be serious and to benefit humanity in some practical way, but allowed us no hint of its dirtiness, intrigue and lustfulness, believing that innocence would be the surest protection against them." Mrs. Graves never talked about war, hoped her boys would become doctors or inventors, and saved and labeled everything in the house carefully, even the jam: "Gooseberry, lemon and rhubarb—a little shop gooseberry added—Nelly reboiled."[1] The world in which Robert Graves and his nine brothers and sisters grew up was a clean, well-ordered one, the world of the English upper classes before 1914.

This world began to change for Graves as he attended a series of English boarding schools, "accumulating unpleasant memories in each" due to his lack of adequate funds, his love of poetry, and his "prudish innocence" about sex. At the final secondary school he attended, Charterhouse, he even feigned insanity so the other boys would leave him alone. He took up boxing during these years as a way of asserting his masculinity, something Hemingway would also do.[2] These adolescent difficulties were not as important as the war, however, in shaping Graves's life. As a young officer with the Royal Welch Fusiliers, Graves was sent to the trenches in France in 1915. Four days before his twenty-first birthday he was seriously wounded by shell fire. For twenty-four hours he was in a coma and left for dead, with shrapnel in his thigh (which almost emasculated him) and in his chest (which nearly killed him). His death had already been announced and a letter of regret sent to his parents when he was found to be alive. Graves later wrote a poem about this experience in which he described himself as descending to the underworld and escaping the jaws of Cerberus [the many-headed dog in classical legend which guards the place] by cramming the monster's mouth full of drugged "army biscuit smeared with ration jam."[3]

His brush with death left its mark. For nearly ten years, he was plagued with lung problems and suffered what was then called "shell shock." In his autobiography, he mentioned nightmares of shells bursting in his bedroom, seeing the faces of friends killed in battle, and an inability to use a telephone or travel by train.[4] Many years later, Graves's friend and fellow poet John Wain wrote that "survival in a death-dealing world" was the innermost theme of Graves's life work as a poet.[5] As a poet, novelist, reviver and translator of classical myths, essayist and playwright, Graves not only described the world lost by the war but affirmed the importance of physical as well as emotional survival. Perhaps not surprisingly, women played an important role in this survival.

The first wife of Robert Graves, Nancy Nicholson, whom he married in January 1918, has been described as "painter, socialist, and vehement feminist." She kept her own name after they married, and they gave their two girls her last name, the two boys his. Marriage to Nancy eventually "wore thin" and they parted company in 1929. Graves spent the next decade with Laura Riding, a very strong willed American woman who influenced his ideas on poetry and moved with him to the Spanish island of Majorca. Laura left Graves in 1939 while he was in the United States in exile from Majorca during World War II. He then married Beryl Hodge, who returned with him to the Spanish island in 1946 and remained there with him until his death.[6] Graves's tendency to idolize strong-willed women heightened or perhaps even inspired his emphasis on the importance of the feminine principle as a creative force for the true poet. In *The White Goddess*, published in 1945, he recalled the great fertility goddess of the matriarchal society which some scholars believe existed in prehistoric times. He then contrasted this figure, the mythical source of passion and feeling, with the god of reason which took men's attention away from nature in later historic times. This prehistoric goddess was a symbol of life for

Graves. While women could certainly be cruel, they were not guilty of organizing wars. By meditating on the White Goddess, poets could come to understand "the true poetic theme, life and death mediated by love."[7] In his long professional life in which he produced over 100 books of fiction, poetry, criticism, and translations, Graves maintained this awareness of the importance of life and death mediated by love. While many of the works he wrote in the late 1920s and early 1930s are witty, irreverent satires poking fun at the hypocritical middle-class world he was saying "Good-bye" to in 1929, Graves was at the same time acclaimed as an old-fashioned romantic poet, fastidious about language and opposed to "the modernist break-up of meter, form, and linguistic decorum."[8] He saw clearly the pretentiousness of the prewar world. Yet he also understood the importance of discipline, courage, and love in keeping the death which he found in the trenches of France from having the last word.

The tension between life and death, between rejection of what was worst in the world and encouragement of the best of which people are capable, can indeed be traced directly back to those French trenches. Fifty years after World War I, in an essay written in the 1960s, Graves recalled the feeling of the front-line soldier, a feeling also described in other World War I era novels and memoirs:

> Trench life was as obsessive as alcohol. Only in the trenches did we feel free—from generals, staff officers, military police, drill-sergeants, . . . journalists, civilian bores, patriots or religious fanatics. . . . But continuous shell fire, and the lesser nuisances of machine guns, trench mortars, rifle grenades, so stimulated our adrenal glands that, after three months, we became mentally off-centre; after six, certifiably insane. We welcomed an occasional ten days leave; but, if lightly wounded, soon grew bored with hospital . . . and schemed to get back again, our wounds half-healed. The trenches made us feel larger than life: only there was death a joke, rather than a threat.[9]

Death could be a joke to a man like Graves, not because it was not real but because he could keep the fear of it under control with a soldier's courage, discipline, and pride—in his comrades and in his job. Since the war itself was so disruptive of traditional values, the soldier's sense of duty became even more important. It is no accident that in all his writing, Graves showed great respect for the soldier, and even an exaggerated admiration for his particular regiment, the Royal Welch Fusiliers. Despite his contempt, shared by many World War I soldiers, for those at home who still thought war glorious, Graves was not a pacifist. When English pacifist Bertrand Russell asked him during the war if he would order his men to fire on munitions-makers who were on strike, Graves said yes, his men "loathe munitions-workers, and would be only too glad . . . to shoot a few. They think that they're all skrimshankers [cowards]." But, Russell exclaimed, don't your men realize "the War's wicked nonsense?" "Yes," Graves replied, "as well as I do." It was a duty to himself, perhaps to his own sanity, which caused him to respond in this way.[10]

Robert Graves could hate war and the near-sighted, selfish leaders who blunder into it, and yet have the greatest respect for those who fight, for they, at least, had to confront life and death as personal realities, not as metaphysical abstractions. His fellow World War I veteran and American literary counterpart, Ernest Hemingway, felt the same way. In an introduction to a 1948 edition of *A Farewell to Arms*, Hemingway, who was in the combat zone in both world wars, explained that he had written so much about war because it was the "constant, bullying, murderous, slovenly crime" of our time. He quickly added, however, that wars are fought "by the finest people that there are" even if they are "made, provoked, and initiated by economic rivalries and by swine that stand to profit from them."[11]

And there were other similarities in the lives and thought of the two men. Hemingway's mother, for example, was as strong-willed and moralistic as Amy Graves. Grace Hemingway believed she gave up a great musical career to marry Ernest's father, an Oak Park, Illinois, physician, in 1896. Mrs. Hemingway would face emotional crises by declaring she had a sick headache and retiring to her room. "Having her wishes crossed always produced a crisis," reported Ernest's younger brother Leicester, "and there were hundreds of them while we children were growing up." Later in life, Ernest *claimed* to hate his mother, and referred to her as "that bitch." She disliked the "words from the gutter" that Ernest put in his books. Amy Graves expressed similar sentiments about the language used by her son in some of his poems. The young Hemingway, like the young Graves, loved his father deeply.[12] Although he was not a combat officer but an ambulance driver on the Italian front, Hemingway was also wounded in World War I. Doctors picked over 200 mortar fragments out of his feet and legs on the eve of his nineteenth birthday. He too suffered "shell shock" and for years was afraid of the dark; he had been wounded at night.[13] Hemingway, like Graves, was involved with a number of women and married four times.

However, despite the similarities in the lives of the two men, their responses to the violence of war and the changes of the postwar world were different. Graves sought physical isolation in Majorca and emotional comfort in the world of the classics and in a search for and promotion of the White Goddess which inspired his love poetry. Hemingway had a far different, more American education for his generation. He never attended college, spent much time hunting and fishing in the woods of Michigan, and met the violence of war and a troubled century with a violent restlessness of his own. While critics dispute the extent to which his short stories and novels are autobiographical, it is certain that many of his heroes do imitate the behavior of their creator: They survive wrenching love affairs, hunt big game, go sports fishing, and generally enjoy what President Theodore Roosevelt (who was in the White House when Hemingway was a young boy) called "the strenuous life." The poetry of Robert Graves is pleasantly reflective, his novels wryly readable, and many of his essays and addresses subtly satirical and smoothly provocative. The prose of Ernest Hemingway is often brilliantly hard, sometimes breathtaking, as befits the journalist he was in his twenties. Hemingway took human courage as his theme, went out of his way to brag about his own courage, and admired it in others. "He lived as he died—violently," his brother wrote. Whether or not his courage failed him at the end is a matter of interpretation. In failing health, Hemingway put a shotgun to his head on July 2, 1961, and used his toe to depress the trigger.[14]

In his fiction, Hemingway dealt more directly than did Graves with the war-related emotional upheavals of the twentieth century. His best novels, *The Sun Also Rises* (1926), *A Farewell to Arms* (1929), and *For Whom the Bell Tolls* (1940), all deal with persons caught up in war or in its cultural aftermath. One critic has described Hemingway's world as "a world at war—war either in the literal sense of armed and calculated conflict, or figuratively as marked everywhere with violence . . . and general hostility:

In his view the hillside is pocked with shell holes, the branch of the tree is shattered, the highway is clogged with soldiers, trucks, refugees . . . and the daughter of the innkeeper has been raped.[15]

In *A Farewell to Arms,* love and death compete for the attention of the reader and the main characters: the American Frederic Henry, an ambulance driver on the Italian front and Catherine Barkley, the nurse he falls in love with in a Milan hospital after he is wounded. During the retreat of the Italian army from Caporetto in 1917, Lieutenant Henry shoots a sergeant who refuses to help him pull his ambulance out of the mud. He is then himself almost killed as a German spy before making a dramatic escape with Catherine to Switzerland. There she dies in childbirth at the end of the novel. The love between Frederic and Catherine is particularly tender by contrast with the confusion and stupidity which surrounds them. But "you never get away with anything," Henry comments when Catherine is in the midst of her doomed labor. Catherine is both brave and optimistic throughout the novel, but the world has to break those with courage: "It kills the very good and the very gentle and the very brave impartially. If you are none of these you can be sure it will kill you too but there will be no special hurry," Henry reflects.[16]

The gloomy picture of Frederic Henry trudging back to his hotel in the rain after Catherine's death emphasizes the bleakness of the world. It does not adequately show us Hemingway's response to this situation. Hemingway's world may be a narrow one circumscribed by violence, "a world seen through a crack in the wall by a man pinned down by gunfire."[17] Yet even a man in that position can continue fighting; most Hemingway heroes do. In *For Whom the Bell Tolls,* the hero, Robert Jordan, sacrifices himself for the good of the group. In the process, he convinces the reader that there are causes that can make one's death worthwhile. Perhaps the best-known struggle against impossible odds in Hemingway's fiction is that of the old Cuban fisherman Santiago in *The Old Man and the Sea* (1952). Down on his luck, Santiago is almost miraculously able to catch a giant marlin. Although he lashes it to his boat, the sharks eat it before he can return home. His dignity and ability to go on make him a symbol of victory in spite of the world's power to defeat him. Santiago is one of a number of Hemingway heroes "who perform valiantly only to have their prizes taken away or scorned."[18]

In his own life, Hemingway sought out the violence and valor with which he often surrounded his characters. "The wound combat makes in you, as a writer, is a very-slow healing one," he once told a correspondent. But Hemingway worked consciously to both write and live his way through the fears left in him by the First World War. He loved taking risks, was preoccupied with death and violence, and continually worked "to prove his adequacy and worth to himself." Believing that "guts" were something that a man either had or did not have, Hemingway rejected the psychiatric theory that we all have a breaking point. While he often exaggerated his own heroism in order to appear more masculine, Hemingway did display personal bravery on occasion. In 1937, he stayed in his Madrid hotel while the city was being shelled during the Spanish Civil War. In Germany during World War II, he was calm in the face of strafing by a German plane and when an artillery shell ripped through the command post where he was eating lunch. Hemingway sought out combat areas during both wars because they gave him a chance to test (or at least brag about) his courage. Hunting trips in Africa and Wyoming served the same purpose. Hemingway also admired bullfighters and before writing *Death in the Afternoon* (1932), he watched the destruction of 1500 bulls.[19]

Hemingway's active life contributed to his literary appeal. He not only seemed to do things that most men lacked the courage or money to do, but he could also write about masculine feats with power and clarity. Even more than Graves, Hemingway believed in the importance of the individual and of the individual's need to assert himself in the face of a civilization which would like to deflate his ego. Like Graves, Hemingway made a living from his writing and found wealth an aid to individual independence. Hemingway used his wealth and freedom to flirt with death in a way Graves found unnecessary. Hemingway once told his World War II comrade Colonel Buck Lanham that he knew death as well as he knew the oldest whore in Havana, where he lived for many years. Although he might buy her a drink, he would never go upstairs with her, he told Lanham. Yet "never is a big word. He knew very well that whatever we say we will never do, we are sure to do sooner or later," one of Hemingway's biographers reflected.[20]

As young men, each of these writers found himself in a near-death situation which forced him to define his values more clearly. Robert Graves and Ernest Hemingway found they hated war but not warriors. "Stay around and they would kill you," Frederic Henry ruefully comments at the end of *A Farewell to Arms*. Neither man wished for that. Graves sought the solace to be found in isolation, poetry, and (for him at least) life-giving mythology. Hemingway comforted himself and others by using words as his weapon against a hostile or potentially hostile world. Both coped with the legacy of destruction bequeathed to us by the wars of this century in different ways. Each, however, forced life and death to meet him on his own terms.

Notes

1. Robert Graves, *Good-bye to All That*, New Edition, Revised (Garden City, NY: Doubleday, 1957), 3–13, 29–30; for a more balanced view of Robert's mother, see Richard Perceval Graves, *Robert Graves: The Assault Heroic 1895–1926* (New York: Viking Penguin, 1990), 5–59.
2. *Ibid.*, 37–41; Katherine Snipes, *Robert Graves* (New York: Frederick Ungar, 1979), 2–3.
3. Snipes, *Robert Graves*, 3; Robert Graves, "Escape" in *Fairies and Fusiliers* (New York: Alfred Knopf, 1918), 76–77.
4. Graves, *Good-Bye to All That*, 287–288, 293.
5. John Wain, "Robert Graves: The Lion in Winter," *New York Times Magazine* (Apr. 1, 1979), 34.
6. Snipes, *Robert Graves*, 5–9; Graves, *Good-Bye to All That*, 343.
7. John B. Vickery, *Robert Graves and the White Goddess* (Lincoln: University of Nebraska Press, 1972), ix–x.
8. Daniel Hoffman, "Graves, Robert (Ranke)," in *Great Writers of the English Language*, edited by James Vinson, Volume II: *Novelists and Prose Writers* (New York: St. Martin's, 1979), 493–498; for a good sample of Graves's earlier irreverent pieces, see Graves, *Occupation: Writer* (London: Cassel and Co., 1951).
9. Graves, "The Kaiser's War," in *Difficult Questions. Easy Answers* (Garden City, NY: Doubleday, 1973), 151.
10. Graves, *Good-bye to All That*, 249; see "The Absentee Fusilier," in *Difficult Questions. Easy Answers*, 164–169, in which Graves discusses his attempt to reenlist during World War II and his tactical and strategic contributions to that war. Several of Graves's historical novels, *Count Belisarius* (1938), *Sergeant Lamb's America* (1940), and *Proceed, Sergeant Lamb* (1941), deal respectfully with military men. See also Martin Seymour Smith, *Robert Graves* (London: Longmans, Green, 1956), 8.
11. Scott Donaldson, *By Force of Will: The Life and Art of Ernest Hemingway* (New York: Viking Press, 1977), 130.

12. Leicester Hemingway, *My Brother Ernest Hemingway* (Cleveland: World Publishing Company, 1962), 21, 37, 42, 93, 100; Donaldson, *By Force of Will*, 292–293; Jeffrey Meyers, *Hemingway: A Biography* (London: Macmillan, 1986), 20–21; Richard Perceval Graves, *Robert Graves: The Years With Laura, 1926–1940* (New York: Viking, 1990), 159.

13. Carlos Baker, *Ernest Hemingway: A Life Story* (New York: Charles Scribner's Sons, 1969), 44–45; Meyers, *Hemingway*, 32, 36, 48; Donaldson, *By Force of Will*, 125–126; Leicester Hemingway, *My Brother Ernest Hemingway*, 56.

14. Leicester Hemingway, *My Brother Ernest Hemingway*, 14.

15. Philip Young, *Ernest Hemingway* (New York: Rinehart and Company, 1952), 214.

16. Ernest Hemingway, *A Farewell to Arms* (New York: Charles Scribner's Sons, 1929), 204, 249, 320.

17. Philip Young, "Ernest Hemingway (1899–1961)," in *American Writers: A Collection of Literary Biographies* (New York: Charles Scribner's Sons, 1974), Volume II, 269.

18. Earl Rovit, *Ernest Hemingway* (New York: Twayne Publishers, 1963), 33; Delbert E. Wylder, *Hemingway's Heroes* (Albuquerque: University of New Mexico Press, 1969), 127–164 and 199–222 for sophisticated discussions of Jordan and Santiago.

19. Lillian Ross, *Portrait of Hemingway* (New York: Simon and Schuster, 1961), 35; Carlos Baker, *Hemingway: A Life Story*, 407–408, 428, 432, 434–435; Meyer, *Hemingway*, 238, 305, 409–411, 545; Richard E. Hardy and John G. Cull, *Hemingway: A Psychological Portrait* (New York: Irvington Publishers, 1988), 31–32; Donaldson, *By Force of Will*, 133–134; Denis Brian, *The Faces of Hemingway: Intimate Portraits of Ernest Hemingway by Those Who Knew Him* (London: Grafton Books, 1988), 17, where a fellow Red Cross volunteer notes that on the trip to Europe during World War I, "everything about [Hemingway] showed he wanted to impress us with his toughness—like spitting over his shoulder." On the connection between Hemingway's early family life and his later need to assert his courage and manliness, see Frederick Crews, "Pressure Under Grace" [a review of Kenneth S. Lynn, *Hemingway* (New York: Simon and Schuster, 1987)] in *The New York Review of Books* (Aug. 13, 1987), 30–37.

20. Baker, *Hemingway: A Life Story*, 432.

Further Reading

MEYERS, JEFFREY. *Hemingway: A Biography* (New York: Harper and Row, 1985). The most readable and best organized of the Hemingway biographies.

GRAVES, ROBERT. *Good-Bye to All That*, New Edition, Revised (Garden City, NY: Doubleday, 1957).

HEMINGWAY, ERNEST. *A Farewell to Arms* (New York: Charles Scribner's Sons, 1929). Considered by many his best novel.

SNIPES, KATHERINE. *Robert Graves* (New York: Frederick Ungar, 1979). Useful short work.

CHAPTER 9

Hearst and Hugenberg: Money, Personality, and Political Power

Can a person "buy" his way into political office? Did political candidates have to appeal to the masses before the age of television?

Two of the firmest beliefs of our age are that political power is the best kind of power to have, and that the best way to get such power is to manipulate the votes of the electorate.

In some modern one-party dictatorships, controlling the electorate is relatively simple. The leaders of the state supply money to the party, and those who depend upon the state for life and livelihood are instructed when, where, and how to vote.

But in states with real elections, where the right to rule or to share in ruling must be won at the ballot box, the problem of how to gain power is much more complicated. For one thing, democratic systems are competitive, and competition, whether for customers or votes, always costs money. In the second place, influencing people to vote for you can be difficult. You must say just the right thing, in the right way, or you can lose your voters. People are fickle and can be angered or lose interest easily. Because this is so, successful campaigning in twentieth-century elections can be largely a matter of "personality."

Just how tricky and expensive the pursuit of political power can be is clear from the careers of two "press lords," William Randolph Hearst (1863–1951) in the United States and Alfred Hugenberg (1865–1951) in Germany. Each of these men owned a chain of newspapers and tried to use his power as a publisher or owner to pursue political ambitions. Both were powerful and wealthy, but both failed politically. Hearst wanted to be president of the United

States; he got no closer than 263 votes at the 1904 Democratic Party convention.[1] Hugenberg wanted to be chancellor of Germany. He succeeded only in helping Adolf Hitler secure that position in 1933. Their failures illustrate both the limitations of wealth and the importance of appealing to the masses in a democratic society.

William Randolph Hearst was born to wealth and it helped determine his personality. By the time of his birth in San Francisco in 1863, his father was part owner of several very productive silver mines in Nevada; he used the earnings from these to buy much California real estate just at the time the transcontinental railroad was beginning to link the west with the rest of the country. "Willie" Hearst, an only child, was indulged by both parents. Growing up he enjoyed "a joyous freedom largely woven out of his mother's ability to accede to his whims." He never learned to deny himself anything, and lacked the sense of proportion that most people acquire as part of the process of growing up emotionally. What Hearst did have was several million dollars. This allowed him to buy most of what he wanted and made it possible for him to postpone maturity for eighty-eight years.[2]

Hearst attended Harvard from 1882 to 1886 but was an indifferent student and was finally expelled for "pranks." Although Hearst and his friends did such things as throw oranges at policemen and carry around a drunken alligator on a leash, he was kicked out in part for organizing a loud, drunken celebration after the election of 1884.[3] Since Hearst had acquired keen interests in both politics and journalism while at Harvard, he then spent a year working as a reporter for the New York *World*, where he came to admire the sensationalistic style of the owner, Joseph Pulitzer. In 1887, the young Hearst persuaded his father to give him complete control of the San Francisco *Examiner*, a paper that his father, now a United States senator, had bought for political purposes.

It was at the *Examiner* and later at the New York *Journal*, which his mother bought for him in 1895, that Hearst contributed to the development of "yellow journalism." This was a deliberate attempt to increase circulation and income by giving poorly educated readers news, drawings, pictures, and headlines that were "startling, amazing, and stupefying." At the time of his death, *Life* magazine wrote an editorial on "Hearst Journalism" explaining what this meant:

He slashed up the front page with scare headlines; he splashed red ink among the black. He filled up the paper with cartoons and photographs, mostly of actresses in bathing suits. He exploited "cheesecake," sex murders, sob stories, comic strips, claptrap science, advice to the lovelorn, the high jinks of high society and invective against political corruption. He threw out the polysyllables and wrote editorials that even a moron could understand.[4]

If the facts were not stupefying and amazing enough, Hearst and his highly paid editors and reporters did not mind making up a few, something that itself would make news today. All this could be relatively harmless if you were merely exaggerating a murder story or inventing a story about a poor orphan who did not really exist. But when Hearst decided to use his yellow journalism as a political weapon, he found that he could change history. And he found that most exhilarating!

Although the young multimillionaire generally supported popular, progressive political measures such as lower gas and water rates, government control of railroads, and popular election of senators, it was his campaign to involve the United States in a war with Spain that has earned him a place (and usually a cartoon) in most American history textbooks.

Hearst had genuine sympathy for the Cuban rebels fighting for their freedom from Spain. Yet he also lacked scruples when it came to whipping up popular American sentiment against the "brutal" Spanish on the island. He sent dozens of reporters to Key West, Florida, as well as to Havana to "cover" the war. Most of them sat in Havana and sent back misleading or false reports about the brave rebels and the cruel Spanish who poisoned wells and drowned prisoners at night. One story, perhaps untrue but symptomatic of the way Hearst operated, notes that when Hearst's artist Frederick Remington sent him a cable in the summer of 1897 saying things were quiet and he wished to come home because there would be no war, Hearst sent him a famous reply: "Please remain. You furnish the pictures and I'll furnish the war."[5] Hearst did just that.

He did it by using his newspapers to enlist thousands of prominent American women in a campaign to secure freedom for a Cuban girl whom he said had been arrested and thrown into a dirty Havana prison for defending her virginity against a Spanish officer.

(She was actually trying to free her father, a rebel, by luring the Spanish colonel to her cottage). He did it by printing Remington's drawings of Cuban girls being stripped and searched by male Spanish officers (again untrue). And finally he did it by loudly accusing the Spanish of blowing up the United States battleship *Maine* in Havana harbor in February 1898. There was no evidence that the Spanish planted the mine that destroyed the ship. Hearst's biographer calls this last "the orgasmic acme of ruthless, truthless" newspaper reporting. But it worked. Congress declared war on Spain on April 19, 1898, by a narrow margin (in the Senate) of forty-two to thirty-five. Hearst's publicity campaign was an important cause of the war fever that led to this vote.[6]

The outbreak of the Spanish-American War demonstrated Hearst's power as a molder of public opinion; in the years to come, he would seek to increase his power and his income by increasing the size of his press empire. At its peak in 1935, the Hearst Organization—really a group of corporations—had newspapers in nineteen cities, including twenty-six dailies and seventeen Sunday editions. These papers accounted for 13.6 percent of the total daily newspaper circulation in the United States. At this time, Hearst also owned several wire services, thirteen magazines, eight radio stations and two motion picture companies.[7]

All this did not satisfy Hearst. Real power in the United States resided in the White House. That is where "W.R." decided he wanted to live, and he pursued this goal for twenty years. Hearst served two terms as a Congressman from New York's eleventh Congressional district from 1903 to 1907, but he never got along with his colleagues, and appeared for only nine rollcall votes in the first two sessions.[8] He unsuccessfully sought the Democratic nomination for president in 1904, the office of mayor of New York City in 1905 and 1909, and the office of governor of New York State (then a stepping-stone to the presidency) in 1906. Although he spent great sums of money in these contests, Hearst's failures in politics only became more dramatic as time went on. In 1908, his third-party candidate for president finished dead last. In 1912, he unsuccessfully opposed Wilson's nomination for president. He confidently predicted that Alf Landon would be elected president in 1936, and in 1948 he pushed the candidacy of General Douglas MacArthur. Hearst's only significant success came in 1932, when he swung the California and Texas delegations to Franklin Roosevelt at the Democratic convention, thus deciding "the convention, the candidate, and the future of the nation." Aside from this one success (which he later regretted), William Randolph Hearst was "the gaudiest failure in American politics."[9]

If Hearst had not been an optimist and a millionaire, these defeats might have crushed his ego. As it was, he consoled himself with frequent trips to Europe, monetary and romantic involvements in Hollywood, the purchase of expensive art objects, and the building and buying of castles at home and abroad. Hearst also became more conservative politically as he aged. From being a supporter of "the people," he became a supporter of big business; from being an advocate of unions, he became their enemy—when the Newspaper Guild began to organize *his* papers; from a proponent of the income tax, he became an opponent—when he realized they were taxing *him!*

Like other men with large egos, the outwardly shy and aloof Hearst tended to see the world in personal terms. He was able to work well only when he could be in charge. For this reason, he managed to anger or alienate all the major political figures with whom he tried to work. His enemies could use his arrogance, inconsistencies, and even his wealth against him. Voters became suspicious of this man who supported "the people" and yet lived like a king. His sincerity was questioned when he opposed United States involvement in the war in Europe in 1915–1917 but supported a war with Mexico when his property there was endangered. Despite his genuine compassion for those who suffered, Hearst could be ruthless in dealing with a political enemy or a wayward employee. All this made him hard to understand, and easy to hate.[10]

All in all, William Randolph Hearst certainly had the money to attain political success; he also had the power of the mass media which, if used skillfully, would have helped him secure elected office. What he lacked was credibility with the voters, and with other power brokers. For a man who could appeal to the masses so successfully in his papers, this was ironic. His fatal flaw was not that he was an egoist, or that he was aloof and difficult to talk with freely. His key weakness was that he was a spoiled brat who flaunted his wealth; that generated jealousy but not votes.

The problems which Alfred Hugenberg faced in his search for political power were different from those encountered by Hearst, despite some general similarities between the two men. Like his

American counterpart, Hugenberg was an arrogant, aloof person who was very sure of his own rightness but who slowly lost touch with his constituents, the voters. Although he owned fewer papers than Hearst (only fourteen), he was able to influence close to two-thirds of the German papers in the 1920s through his subscription service, which supplied news, features, and political opinions to about 1900 of the 3000 papers in that country.[11] Hugenberg's views were far different from those of Hearst, as Imperial Germany was different from Progressive era America.

Perhaps the most important difference between the two men is that whereas Hearst's political views changed during his life, Alfred Hugenberg was a consistent believer in conservative capitalism and German expansion. Although the young Alfred had some poetic pretensions, formed a poetry club while in school in Hanover, and published a collection of poems with a friend in 1886,[12] he soon settled down to the study of economics and defined his lifelong convictions. These began and ended with praise of the free market economy and condemnation of Marxism and socialism in all forms. The state, he believed, should encourage economic competition and be willing to expand the amount of land available to farmers and business people—by conquest if necessary. In 1890, Hugenberg was one of the founders of the Pan-German League, a group of aggressive imperialists who wanted to gather all Germanic peoples into one large state.[13] In pursuit of these goals, Hugenberg became a civil servant during the 1890s. However, since the pre-World War I German government was not as rigorously capitalistic as he was and would not confiscate aristocratic estates in eastern Germany and turn them over to small farmers, who he felt would work them more efficiently, he resigned. Hugenberg worked on a bank board in Frankfurt for a time and in 1909 became chairman of the board of the famous Krupp munitions firm in Essen. While there he pursued a plan to give company-sponsored homes to the workers. Since the workers chose to improve their conditions by joining unions instead, little came of the plan.[14]

When World War I broke out, Hugenberg was among those who supported Germany's expansionist war aims. To avoid the growth of socialism, he believed, workers had to be compensated with land. German industry also needed raw materials and markets and, given the early successes of the German army during the war, it seemed easy to secure this land from the French, the Belgians, and the Russians. The fact that these war aims became outdated by 1917 when the war had become a stalemate failed to embarrass Hugenberg or his industrialist friends at all.

Despite Germany's defeat in the war, Hugenberg changed none of his prewar views. He and his fellow industrialists, most of them Ruhr Valley coal or steel magnates, did decide that they had to cope with the democratic Weimar Republic established in Germany. They did this by establishing a political party, the German National People's Party (Nationalist Party) and by setting up a number of corporations which would allow industrialists to quietly funnel money into the media to influence public opinion. Hugenberg and his associates purchased a major Berlin publishing house run by August Scherl. This Scherl organization published two major dailies, various weekly papers, and periodicals. Hugenberg also helped begin the Reich Association of German Industry, a lobbying group which provided secret funds to a number of right-wing, counterrevolutionary or antirepublican organizations.[15]

During the 1920s the Hugenberg newspapers, and those who subscribed to his wire services, worked hard to convince Germans of the evil unfairness of the Versailles Treaty restrictions, especially the heavy reparations payments, placed on Germany after World War I. Hugenberg's papers and his party were, however, generally unwilling to work with the government on a positive program to remove treaty restrictions. Other moderate conservatives, such as Gustav Stresemann of the German People's Party, adopted a policy of "fulfillment" by the mid-1920s. By being cooperative and working with the French and the British to pay reparations, the Germans could show their goodwill, Stresemann believed, and more quickly get the hated treaty revised.

Hugenberg would have none of this; he insisted that any form of "collaboration" would simply aid the socialists and Germany's Marxist enemies at home and abroad. His radical right-wing views slowly alienated his industrialist colleagues. His insistence on Germany's need for autarchy [economic self-sufficiency] and his total opposition to all unions was hardly realistic. While other right-wing politicians still paid lip service to some of these goals in order to get votes, Hugenberg really believed in them.[16]

The Depression came to Hugenberg's aid by causing many Germans, whose political immaturity had been encouraged by the Hugenberg press, to espouse extremist solutions to Germany's economic problems. In 1928, a year before the great stock market crash in the United States, Hugenberg was able to wrest control of the Nationalist Party from its more moderate leader, Count Kuno Westarp. The following year, Hugenberg began his fateful policy of cooperating with other, more popular right-wing groups in an effort to destroy the Weimar Republic.

The attempted referendum in 1929 to stop the German government from endorsing the Young Plan, which scaled down Germany's reparations payments—and thus strengthened the hand of the hated republican government—was a failure. However, during this campaign Hugenberg allied with the National Socialist Party of Adolf Hitler and gave Hitler's movement invaluable publicity in the Hugenberg newspapers. Hugenberg thought he was merely using Hitler, that the mad antisemitic ravings of the popular Nazi orator could be helpful in preparing voters to accept the "proper" conservative rule of Hugenberg and his Nationalist Party colleagues. He was sadly mistaken.

Aided by Hugenberg's publicity and conservative funds on occasion, the Nazi party made spectacular electoral gains from 1930 to 1932. They increased their number of Reichstag [national legislature] representatives from 12 to 107 in the general election of September 1930, and gained 230 seats in the Reichstag in July of 1932. The number of seats held by Hugenberg's party declined in each of these elections. Hitler's actual assumption of the chancellorship in January 1933 was not entirely Hugenberg's fault. Other conservatives, especially General Kurt von Schleicher and Franz von Papen, blinded as was Hugenberg to the radical aims and ruthlessness of Hitler, made behind-the-scene deals which allowed Hitler to come to power in Germany on January 30. However, Hugenberg's stubborn refusal to work with moderates in Germany made him responsible "in a special way" for the instability of the Weimar Republic.[17] This instability allowed Hitler to assume power and, like Hearst's support of Franklin Roosevelt, helped change the course of modern history.

Historians are fond of using words like "unscrupulous" and "ambitious" to describe both Hearst and Hugenberg, and with good reason.[18] These were very influential men, able to use vast sums of money to win the support and change the minds of millions of people. Yet in the final analysis both failed, even in their chosen fields. Hearst was not a good newspaperman because he violated a cardinal rule of journalism—to tell the truth—so often in his pages. And Hugenberg was not a good politician because he refused to compromise ninety-eight percent of the time—and compromise is a cardinal rule of politics. And if Hugenberg's ideology was out of date politically, so was his dress. His "brush-cut hair, handlebar mustache, and high, Victorian collar" caused many Berliners to mockingly call him "The Hamster."[19] His appearance was as much of a political liability to him as Hearst's arrogance and shyness in public were to him. The lesson might be that in a state with popularly elected leaders, "money isn't everything." That fact is not by itself an endorsement of the wisdom of the democratic system, for the crucial element that must go along with money—call it "personality" or "charisma"—is even harder to rationally assess than the impact of money. Ask those Germans who have been trying for half a century to explain the success of Hitler in Germany.

Notes

1. W. A. Swanberg, *Citizen Hearst: A Biography of William Randolph Hearst* (New York: Charles Scribner's Sons, 1961), 218.
2. Swanberg, *Ibid.*, 10, 24, 526; George B. West, "Hearst: A Psychological Note," in Edwin Emery and Edwin Hopkins, editors, *Highlights in the History of the American Press* (Minneapolis: University of Minnesota Press, 1954), 300–316.
3. Swanberg, *Citizen Hearst*, 24–29.
4. Swanberg, *Ibid.*, 45; *Life*, Aug. 27, 1951, 22.
5. Swanberg, *Citizen Hearst*, 107–108, 110; see also "Hearst Didn't Send Cable to Remington," by Dom Bonafede in *New York Times*, Aug. 1, 1991, A20. This letter to the editor notes that Remington never mentioned such a cable, Hearst flatly denied ever sending one, and the only source for this is the memoirs of James Creelman, a journalist who worked for Hearst.
6. Swanberg, *Citizen Hearst*, 111–112, 120–144.
7. Edwin Emery, "William Randolph Hearst: A Tentative Appraisal," in *Highlights*, 320.
8. Swanberg, *Citizen Hearst*, 208–218.
9. Louis Untermeyer, "William Randolph Hearst," in *Makers of the Modern World* (New York: Simon and Schuster, 1955), 311–320; see Swanberg, *Citizen Hearst*, 288, 436–437.
10. Swanberg, *Citizen Hearst*, 297, 359.

11. John A. Leopold, *Alfred Hugenberg: The Radical Nationalist Campaign against the Weimar Republic* (New Haven: Yale University Press, 1977), 13–15.

12. Heidrun Holzbach, *Das "System Hugenberg": Die Organisation bürgerlicher Sammlungs-politik vor dem Aufstieg der NSDAP* (Stuttgart: Deutsche Verlags-Anstalt, 1981), 21–23.

13. Leopold, *Alfred Hugenberg*, 6.

14. *Ibid.*, 1–3.

15. *Ibid.*, 8–12.

16. *Ibid.*, 37–38, 41; D. P. Walker, "The German Nationalist People's Party: The Conservative Dilemma in the Weimar Republic," *Journal of Contemporary History*, 14, October 1979, 641–642.

17. Holzbach, *Das "System Hugenberg,"* 25; Leopold, *Alfred Hugenberg*, 172–173.

18. See William Halperin, *Germany Tried Democracy: A Political History of the Reich from 1918 to 1933* (New York: Thomas Crowell, 1946), 293; Peter Gay, *Weimar Culture: The Outsider as Insider* (New York: Harper and Row, 1968), 133.

19. Leopold, *Alfred Hugenberg*, 105.

Further Reading

LEOPOLD, JOHN A. *Alfred Hugenberg: The Radical Nationalist Campaign Against the Weimar Republic* (New Haven: Yale University Press, 1977). The only good work in English.

SWANBERG, W. A. *Citizen Hearst: A Biography of William Randolph Hearst* (New York: Charles Scribner's Sons, 1961). Best biography.

TEBBEL, JOHN. *The Life and Good Times of William Randolph Hearst* (New York: E. P. Dutton, 1952). Fun to read.

CHAPTER 10

Eva Perón and Golda Meir: Helping the Dispossessed— Two Models

How did the personalities of two female leaders affect the way they chose to help the dispossessed in their two very different cultural communities? Is power best exercised in formal or informal ways?

In the twentieth century more people have been forced into poverty or homelessness by wars, revolutions, and economic inequalities than ever before, and private and public efforts to help such people have increased correspondingly.

The lives of two twentieth-century women, Eva Perón of Argentina (1919–1952) and Golda Meir of Israel (1898–1978) illustrate two vastly different ways of aiding the dispossessed. Eva Perón was the wife of the president of Argentina, Juan Perón, and his "ambassador" to the poor, or *descamisados* ("shirtless ones"), from 1946 to her death in 1952. Golda Meir spent much of her life working for the Zionist [Jewish nationalist] movement in Palestine before serving as minister of labor, foreign minister, and, finally, prime minister of the state of Israel from 1969 to 1974.

Both of these powerful, determined women helped the dispossessed. Eva Perón, still a legendary figure in Argentina, did it by creating what *Time* magazine called "the splashiest giveaway machine the world ever saw."[1] Meir, who seemed to some to be the archetypal Jewish grandmother, helped her people by working to establish an independent state characterized by strong social welfare institutions. Their quite different approaches to social justice grew out of the different histories and cultures of the Jewish and Argentine peoples as well as from the very different personalities of these two women.

Any comparison of them is made more difficult by the controversial nature of Eva Perón's career as well as by a general North American ignorance of Latin American political traditions. North Americans tend to be more sympathetic to a leader like Golda Meir because she adopted a policy of national self-determination and a social welfare ideology more familiar in the United States. Eva Perón's behavior, by contrast, is not only unfamiliar; it also seems less rational. Golda Meir strikes us as better organized, employing public institutions in the pursuit of her cause; Eva Perón, on the other hand, was charismatic [having personal magnetism or charm] and spontaneous, depending on personal power, rather than on institutions, to reach her goals. Of the two, Eva was the more fascinating.

Born the illegitimate daughter of Juana Ibarguren and Juan Duarte in the small village of Los Toldos, Eva watched her mother struggle to feed five children after the death of her father when Eva was six. Early she was aware of the pain of being poor. When she and her four illegitimate siblings walked twenty miles to attend her father's funeral, they were initially turned away by the wealthier "legal" family and only allowed to attend when the mayor intervened. Years later she wrote in her autobiography that she "was sad for many days when I first realized that there were poor and rich in the world; . . . the fact of the existence of the poor did not hurt me so much as the knowledge that, at the same time, the rich existed."[2]

At age fifteen, Eva went to Buenos Aires, then the third-largest city in the western hemisphere, to become an actress. Exactly how she got there and what she did after she arrived is uncertain; Evita ("little Eva," the nickname by which she became famous later) spoke little about her early life. She had her birth certificate changed so she would appear legitimate, and she distorted much of what she did reveal. Her enemies accused her of being a prostitute during her early years in the capital, and she did have a number of lovers. But it is more likely that she earned a meager living through a series of temporary acting jobs with traveling companies until she was able to achieve moderate success as a radio actress in the early 1940s.[3]

Eva Duarte's life changed dramatically in January of 1944 when she became the mistress of Colonel Juan Perón, minister of labor and soon-to-be minister of war in the military government which had come to power eighteen months earlier. In the former position, he appealed to Argentine workers (and undercut the Communist and Socialist union leaders) by organizing government-sponsored unions which raised salaries and increased benefits for the workers, whose interests had been ignored by previous liberal governments. As minister of war, he maintained the support of conservatives in the army by assuring them that the privileges he was granting workers were "strictly limited by the powers of the State."[4]

Despite these assurances, it was plain that—true to the Latin American political tradition—Perón was empowering the workers in order to build a personal power base, independent of the military. When new laws guaranteeing higher wages or shorter hours were proposed or signed, the minister of labor himself announced the proposal or signed the bill. During strikes, Perón personally visited the strikers and was photographed listening to their complaints, and he often took to the radio to announce such things as new health insurance or retirement benefits. Argentina was still a country of huge cattle ranches, and towns were often hundreds of miles apart. The rural poor who migrated to Buenos Aires in large numbers during the first half of the twentieth century were accustomed not to democracy but to rule by local strongmen *(caudillos)* who governed—often extralegally—by establishing a personal bond with their people. By courting the previously neglected urban workers, Juan Perón successfully appealed to this populist, personalist tradition.[5] His mistress Evita would later, as his wife, use this tradition in a particularly feminine way to make her mark on history.

Before this could happen, Juan Perón had to become the sole ruler of Argentina. By 1945, Perón, who had added the title of vice-president in late 1944, was clearly the most powerful of the military leaders. Fear of his growing power led the other generals to demand Perón's resignation on October 9, 1945, citing as a reason that he lived openly with his mistress, Evita. After his resignation and a farewell speech to employees at the Ministry of Labor (which he cleverly had broadcast on the radio), Perón was imprisoned. Later Peronist propaganda claims that during the next week, Evita went to the working-class neighborhoods in Buenos Aires and rallied union leaders who encouraged 300,000 workers, derisively called "shirtless ones" by the conservative press, to descend on the central square in the capital to demand the release of Perón.[6] [*Descamisados* did not wear jackets; they were not literally shirtless.] Eva encouraged Perón not to give up while throngs of workers, fearing the loss of Perón would mean the loss of their recent benefits, took over the city and gathered in the Plaza de Mayo on October 17. Overwhelmed by the size of the crowd organized by Perón's supporters in the unions and at the Ministry of Labor, the military leaders released Perón from prison that night. He gave an impromptu speech from the balcony of the presidential palace, announcing that he would run for president in the next general election. Perón married Evita five days later and won the election of February 1946 with fifty-two percent of the vote. He won a second term as president in 1951 by an even larger margin and retained power until 1955 by implementing a policy of economic nationalism (buying back utilities and industries from foreigners, especially the British) which appealed to both the army and the organized working class. Within a year of her husband's first election, Evita was playing a key role—some say she overshadowed him—in keeping working-class support.

She did this primarily through her creation (almost by accident) of what became known as the "Eva Perón Foundation." The wealthy upper-class women of Buenos Aires who ran the country's largest private charity organization refused to invite Eva to lead the benevolence society, a customary role for the President's wife, because of her lower-class background. So Evita began her own Social Aid, or Welfare, Foundation, which later took her name. Within four years, it became a massive welfare organization. By 1951, the foundation had built 1000 schools, 600 new homes, and 60 hospitals, and it was training 1300 nursing students a year and would open 35 clinics that year alone. By this time, it had assets of over $200 million, 14,000 permanent employees, including thousands of construction workers, and even a staff of priests.[7]

What made Eva's foundation unique was that although it was one woman's personal patronage system, it was a semiofficial one, supported with both voluntary and semicoerced private funds and outright government grants. Business leaders were "expected" to contribute; one who did not had his factory closed for several years for violations of health regulations. When new collective bargaining agreements were signed, union members "donated" the first month's salary increase to the foundation. It also received twenty percent of the proceeds from the national lottery and other state revenues.[8]

Despite its semiofficial nature, the foundation was run by Evita in an extremely personal fashion; she encouraged people to write her directly about their problems, and she claimed to receive thousands of letters each day. Several times a week, in the fashion of the monarchs of old Spain, she granted audiences to the poor of her "kingdom." She talked to the destitute for hours at a time in her office, giving them everything from homes and shoes to cooking pots and cash. Although this was stage-managed, with floodlights over her desk and photographers present, witnesses reported that she was genuinely kind to all she met and interested in their problems. Father Hernán Benítez, her confessor, present at many of these sessions, said later: "I saw her kiss the leprous. I saw her kiss those who were suffering from tuberculosis or cancer. I saw her distribute . . . a love that rescues charity, removing that burden of injury to the poor that charity implies."[9] Indeed, Evita despised the idea of charity, which she believed placed an obligation on the recipients and gave the upper-class "oligarchs," as they were called in Argentina, a sense of superiority. She regarded her gifts as social justice, as "reparations" for past wrongs inflicted on the lower classes. For that reason, she insisted on attractive interior decorations in her hospitals and children's homes and often used expensive materials such as marble in their construction. She believed the poor deserved it. In a published series of lectures and in her autobiography, largely written by others but reflecting her views, she wrote that many of the social welfare buildings she saw in Europe "are cold and poor. Many have been built according to the standards of the rich . . . and when the rich think of the poor, they think poorly. Others have been erected by State standards; and the State can only build bureaucratically, that is . . . with coldness, from which love is lacking."[10] We could have no clearer expression of the personalist Latin American political culture which produced both Evita and her "reform."

Given this genuine sympathy for the poor, especially when combined with her beauty, dedication to working long hours, and skillful self-promotion, it is not surprising that many poor Argentines began to see Evita as a holy person, "the Lady of Hope" (a title created by a newspaper she owned) who was giving her life for the poor. She was literally working herself to death. Months before her early death from uterine cancer on July 26, 1952, something she could have avoided by agreeing to surgery thirty months earlier, she was being referred to as a "saint" by many Argentines. Shortly before her death the Peronist-dominated legislature voted her the title of "Spiritual Chief of the Nation." While much of this myth of "Saint Evita" was consciously contrived to gain support for the government, there is some evidence that Eva herself was changed by her contact with the poor and that she came to believe or even transcend the Peronist propaganda. The president's wife who, on a "goodwill" trip to Europe in 1947, had worn so much expensive fur and jewelry that she alienated many Europeans, in her last years wore less jewelry and more sober business suits while working nearly full-time at the foundation. "Her work acquired the importance and sanctity of a 'mission.' . . . Even when she was exhausted and obviously ill, she continued to work. Of all the many distortions surrounding her life the least outrageous and closest to the truth is the suggestion that she elected to die for Perón and Peronism." During her final two years of life, she appears to have accepted her own "martyrdom" by "increasing her activity to levels that would have been sustained with difficulty even by a healthy person."[11]

This view of Eva Perón is controversial because many see it as based on propaganda by a dictatorial regime that jailed its political opponents, ended press freedoms, and reshaped the political system to eliminate opposition parties. In her speeches and written works, Evita's sentimental exaggeration of Juan Perón's virtues certainly reads like propaganda. He was a "genius," a "meteor that burns to illuminate our age," a man with "no defects," yet "humble even to the smallest detail." Perón is compared to Christ and Napoleon, and Evita claims to be "the shadow of the Leader," a person willing "to give her life [for him] at any time," and "a link stretched between the hopes of the people and the fulfilling hands of Perón."[12] Only by appreciating the importance of the personal bond between a leader and his (or her, in this case) followers in the Latin American *caudillo* tradition can we begin to understand the success of the Peróns— and the enduring quality of the myth of Evita.

Although Eva Perón could be vindictive toward enemies and to those who failed to flatter her sufficiently—it was said that one young man was jailed for not donating his radio quiz show winnings to the foundation—historians disagree on whether she sought power for herself or was only "the shadow of the Leader." Perón made her the *de facto* head [leader "in fact" though not "in law"—*de jure*] of the Ministry of Labor (the official minister was José Freire) where she purged all labor leaders not completely subservient to Perón. Evita also supported women's suffrage, a reality by 1948, and organized the Peronist Women's Party in 1949 to mobilize women's votes for Perón. Two million women voted in the 1951 presidential election, contributing to Perón's victory margin. Evita was not a feminist, however. She claimed that most feminists wanted to make women too much like men, and she wrote that women "suffer from love more than men."[13] Neither in her work with the labor unions nor with women did Eva do anything to suggest that she was trying to upstage her husband. Only in 1951, when she tolerated a popular campaign by the workers' organizations to put her on the ballot as a vice-presidential candidate, did the question of whether she was seeking power for herself arise. After she was pressured by a crowd on August 22 to accept the nomination, she appeared to do so by saying, "I will do what the people say." Perón, aware that the army would not accept a female commander-in-chief, told her to refuse, which she did ten days later. By this time she was already so ill that she was forced to spend most of her remaining months of life in bed. In sum, there is little evidence that Evita sought power for herself; most of her activities suggest that she did, in fact, see herself as Perón's "shadow."

Yet Evita remains a legend. Whether people loved her or hated her, whether she was the "lady of hope" or "the great whore" (*la gran puta*), the charismatic nature of Evita's power stirred emotions outside the boundaries of formal legal bureaucratic authority. Her supporters saw her bond with them as one of love; her middle- and upper-class enemies saw her power as "mystical, irrational, impulsive, [and] disordered."[14]

One way to gauge public perceptions of Eva Perón and Golda Meir (in the United States at least) is to review obituary notices. *Time* magazine's obituary for Evita was entitled "Cinderella from the Pampas"; *Newsweek* called her a "tough, indefatigable" woman who "tied thousands around her much beringed finger." *Life* admitted she had become "the most powerful woman in the western hemisphere" but also belittled her as "the most spectacular Cinderella girl of her time." Only *The New York Times* avoided flippancy and referred to her as Perón's "most faithful and trusted collaborator" who exerted "tremendous power" even from her sickbed. In contrast, when Golda Meir died in 1978, *The New York Times* honored the former prime minister of Israel with two full pages which included many references to her toughness, sense of humor, and use of plain language. *Time* called her "a tough maternal legend" and American conservative commentator William F. Buckley asked that "God be with her. She will look after Him."[15]

It is not surprising that Golda Meir is treated with greater seriousness by journalists and historians. The two women were a world apart geographically, philosophically, and temperamentally. If Eva's brief career demonstrates the impact of charismatic leadership on the long-term *memory* of a Latin American people, Golda Meir's much longer career demonstrates how a life of commitment to institutionalizing an idea can contribute to long-term *change* for a people. Like Eva Perón, she was not willing to accept the lot of the dispossessed—Jews without a state in this case—but unlike her, Meir wanted to create an environment and state in Palestine that would guarantee the Jewish dispossessed long-term security.

Golda Mabrovitch was born in Russia and could remember her father boarding up the family home in Kiev after he had been warned of a pogrom [attack on Jews, often government-sponsored]. She recalled thinking that maybe Jews should move to a place where the government would not let this happen. The Mabrovitch family moved to the United States in 1906, and she finished high school in Milwaukee after spending some time with her sister and brother-in-law in Denver. Her energy and organizational skills were shown as early as age eleven when she organized a group of class-mates who secured the donation of a hall, knocked on doors, and painted posters asking parents to attend a meeting where she gave a speech pleading for money to buy school books (public school in Milwaukee was free; books were not). While in high school, Meir led a fund-raising effort for Jewish workers in Palestine before de-ciding to join the movement to establish a Jewish state in Palestine [Zionism], a cause to which she devoted her life. "The Jews must have a land of their own again—and I must help build it, not by making speeches or raising funds, but by living and working there [in Palestine]."[16] But first she had to convince her boyfriend, Morris Meyerson, to go with her. She would not marry him until he did. They were married in 1917 but it was not until May 1921 that the Meyersons and a small group of fellow adventurers boarded the barely seaworthy *S.S. Pocahontas* for the long journey to Palestine. When they finally arrived at the barren, wind-swept railroad sta-tion on the edge of the frontier city of Tel Aviv, one member of the party said jokingly: "Well, Goldie, you wanted to come to Eretz Yis-roel [the land of Israel]. Here we are. Now we can all go back—it's enough." She was not amused.[17]

She and Morris plunged into the life of agricultural workers at the Merhavia kibbutz in the valley of Jezreel. The kibbutzim were farming communes established on usually poor or swampy land not previously cultivated. By living on the land and sharing hard work and their few possessions, these Jewish pioneers hoped to build a Jewish community in Palestine; they wished to "redeem" them-selves and the land at the same time. Such workers made it possible for the state of Israel to support over a million immigrants by 1951.

Although Golda loved Merhavia, Morris disliked communal living and did not want to have children there since kibbutz children were raised in nurseries and not exclusively by their parents. When he took ill in 1923 the couple moved to Tel Aviv and then Jerusalem. Two children, Menachem and Sarah, were born in the 1920s, and during these years Mrs. Meyerson lived as an impoverished housewife, taking in laundry to pay Sarah's nursery school fees. The poverty bothered her less than being isolated from the important political and social work being done around her: "Instead of actively helping build the Jewish national home . . . I found myself cooped up in a tiny apartment in Jerusalem, all my thoughts and energy concentrated on making do with Morris' wages." Frustrated, she finally accepted a position working for the General Federation of Jewish Labor (Histadrut), and this led to her separation from her husband. Despite "bitter regret" at the failure of her marriage and the "inner struggles and despairs" of a working mother, Meir [the Hebrew form of Meyerson] remained an active, full-time worker in Histadrut and Mapai [the Labor Party] the rest of her life.[18]

One of the clearest differences between Eva Perón and Golda Meir is that Evita's career was possible because of her marriage and intense support for her husband, while Meir's career was made possible by the failure of her marriage. Morris, more poet than politician, had not wanted her to join the Zionist movement in the first place.[19] Another clear difference, of course, is that Eva started at the top in her attempt to help the less fortunate in her society; Meir spent many years working her way through a number of Zionist organizations before becoming the leader of her people.

From 1932 to 1934, Meir was back in the United States giving speeches and raising money for rebuilding in Palestine. In 1934 she joined the executive committee of Histadrut, and within a few years was in charge of mutual aid funds for all Jewish workers in Palestine. In 1937 it was back to the USA to raise money to build a Jewish harbor in Tel Aviv when the British, who controlled Palestine as a "mandate" from the League of Nations, closed the harbor at Jaffa after Arab riots in 1936.

By the late 1930s, the outline of future Arab-Jewish conflict was emerging. Arabs feared and resented Jewish immigration to Palestine. On the other hand, Hitler's persecution of German Jews made clear to the *yishuv* [Jewish community in Palestine] that many more Jews from Europe needed a place of refuge. The British, in charge of Palestine, tried to slow Jewish immigration to Palestine in order to please the Arabs. Jews felt betrayed because the British in 1917, during World War I, had promised the Zionists "a Jewish homeland" in Palestine. But the language of this promise, in the form of the Balfour Declaration, did not promise a national state; it was deliberately and diplomatically vague.

Continued British refusal to allow free Jewish entry into Palestine during World War II, and even after 1945 when the extent of the Holocaust [destruction of six million Jews in Europe by the Nazis] became known, made it inevitable that Jews would fight the British, if necessary, to create their own state. In 1946, testifying before an Anglo-American Committee of Inquiry examining the question of Jewish immigration to Palestine, Meir described the two goals that motivated her and most other Jewish workers in Palestine: to create "an independent Jewish life in the Jewish homeland" and "to create a new society . . . of equality, justice, and cooperation." Socialist economic organization, such as that found in the kibbutzim, and national political independence were goals of these soon-to-be Israelis. Both, as well as humanitarian concern for the survivors of Hitler's death camps, required unrestricted Jewish immigration.[20]

No one was surprised that Meir, by then a leading member of the Labor Party, was one of the signers of the Israeli declaration of independence in May 1948, written after the Arab nations rejected the United Nations plan to partition Palestine into separate Jewish and Arab states. During the previous months, to prepare for the expected Arab attempts to destroy the new state, Meir raised fifty million dollars among American Jews for military supplies. When she returned home, David Ben-Gurion, Israel's first prime minister, said that "someday when history will be written, it will be said that there was a Jewish woman who got the money which made the state possible."[21]

In 1948, when Eva Perón was expanding the work of her foundation, Golda Meir was serving her new state as its first ambassador to Moscow. A year later, she became minister of labor in the Israeli cabinet. While Perón was building hundreds of schools and dozens of hospitals for the Argentine poor, Meir was feeding, housing, and finding jobs for nearly 700,000 new immigrants who had poured into Israel by 1951. In 1949 her ministry began to build 30,000 housing units; she also organized a large road-building program.[22]

As Israeli foreign minister in 1956, Meir had to defend her country's preemptive strike against the Arab armies massing on its borders in October of that year. "If hostile forces gather for our proposed destruction," she explained, "they must not demand that we provide them with ideal conditions for the realization of their plans." This is only one example of Golda Meir's tough language. When asked about the possibility of compromise with the Arabs after a later war, in 1967, she responded: "The Arabs wish us dead. We want to live. That's very hard to compromise."[23]

Up through her period of service as prime minister, which included the Yom Kippur war of 1973, Meir continued to think of herself as a "leader who was a woman rather than a woman leader." When someone asked her how it felt to be a woman minister, she replied: "I don't know. I was never a man minister." On another occasion when the cabinet was discussing an outbreak of assaults on women at night, one member of a conservative religious group suggested a curfew for women after dark. Meir remarked: "But it's the men who are attacking the women. If there is to be a curfew, let the men stay at home, not the women."[24] Meir's attitude toward women and her language, like her method of helping the poor, were as rationally straightforward as those of her Argentine counterpart were sentimental.

In her autobiography Golda Meir noted with pride that the Jewish population of Palestine had grown from 80,000 people in 1921 to over three million in 1975. She also expressed her belief that Israel would someday find peace with her neighbors, but added that "no one will make peace with a weak Israel. If Israel is not strong, there will be no peace."[25]

Despite continuing hostility in Arab-Israeli relations in the years since Golda Meir's death, it is clear that many Jews have found a measure of security in the Jewish state thanks to the systematic efforts at nation building by her and her Labor Party colleagues. Although Eva Perón's memory still lives in Argentina, and helped inspire a revolutionary movement in the 1970s, it is more difficult to see the lasting effects of her work. Inflation eroded the economic gains made by the poor under the Peróns in the late 1940s. Three years after Evita's death, Juan Perón was overthrown in a military coup and although the Peronist party remained active and was even able to bring Juan Perón back as president in 1973 till his death in 1974, the work of Evita in helping the dispossessed of her country left few concrete results. But then the goals of these two strong women were quite different. Golda Meir wanted the Jews of the world to know there was one place where they would be safe and could feel at home. She succeeded in helping to create such a place. Andrew Lloyd Webber and Tim Rice, in their 1978 musical, "Evita," have the title character say that she was not concerned with the repressive side of her government; she was "in business . . . to give all my *descamisados* a magical moment or two." If this was her goal, she too succeeded.

Notes

1. *Time,* Aug. 4, 1952, 33. Eva Perón will be referred to as Eva or Evita throughout this chapter to avoid confusing her with her husband.
2. Eva Perón, *My Mission in Life,* trans. by Ethel Cherry (New York: Vantage Press, 1953), 6.
3. The most balanced account of this period in Eva's life is found in Nicholas Fraser and Marysa Navarro, *Eva Perón* (New York: Norton, 1980), 20–27; see also John Barnes, *Evita: First Lady. A Biography of Eva Perón* (New York: Grove Press, 1978), 20–22.
4. Fraser and Navarro, *Eva Perón,* 40.
5. Robert Crassweller, *Perón and the Enigmas of Argentina* (New York: Norton, 1987), 120, 223; Robert J. Alexander, *Juan Domingo Perón: A History* (Boulder, CO: Westview Press, 1979), 37–39; Susan and Peter Calvert, *Argentina: Political Culture and Instability* (Pittsburgh: University of Pittsburgh Press, 1989), 80–84; Glen Caudill Dealy, *The Latin Americans: Spirit and Ethos* (Boulder, CO: Westview Press, 1992), 58–61.
6. See Eva Perón, *My Mission,* 27–28, 30.
7. Barnes, *Evita,* 14; Crassweller, *Enigmas,* 209–210; Richard Bourne, "Eva Perón," in *Political Leaders of Latin America* (New York: Alfred A. Knopf, 1970), 270.
8. Fraser and Navarro, *Eva Perón,* 119; Alexander, *Perón,* 83; Crassweller, *Enigmas,* 210.
9. Fraser and Navarro, *Eva Perón,* 122–126; Eva Perón, *My Mission,* 117–119.
10. Eva Perón, *History of Peronism* (Buenos Aires: Servicio Internacional Publicaciones Argentinas, [1952]), 188–189; *My Mission,* 125–126, 144, 154–159.
11. Fraser and Navarro, *Eva Perón,* 125, 135; J. M. Taylor, *Eva Perón: The Myths of a Woman* (Chicago: University of Chicago Press, 1979), 57.
12. Eva Perón, *History of Peronism,* 12, 28–29, 56, 104, 141; *My Mission,* 61, 80, 176.
13. Barnes, *Evita,* 74–76; Eva Perón, *My Mission,* 51, 185.
14. See Taylor, *Myths of a Woman,* 11–19, 86–87, 104. She suggests that Eva's power was not only personal but also different from the personal power of her husband, because the personal, extralegal power of a

woman stirs different fears in a macho, male-dominated society like that in Latin America than does the same extralegal power when exercised by a man. See also Marysa Navarro, "Evita's Charismatic Leadership," in *Latin American Populism in Comparative Perspective,* edited by Michael L. Conniff (Albuquerque: University of New Mexico Press, 1982), 47–66, for a summary of how Evita "moved outside of the institutional structure."

15. *Time,* Aug. 4, 1952, 33; Dec. 18, 1978, 43–43; *Newsweek,* Aug. 4, 1952, 47; *Life,* Aug. 4, 1952, 32; *The New York Times,* July 27, 1952, 56; Dec. 9, 1978, 6–7; *The National Review,* Jan. 5, 1979, 18.

16. Marie Syrkin, *Golda Meir: Israel's Leader* (New York: G. P. Putnam's Sons, 1969), 14–37; Ralph G. Martin, *Golda: A Biography* (New York: Ballantine Books, 1990), 7–8, 12–13, 33–34, 44–45, 59, 63; Golda Meir, *My Life* (New York: G. P. Putnam's Sons, 1975), 22–25, 63. Golda Meir's married name was Meyerson, only changed to the Hebrew Meir in 1956 as a requirement for serving in the Israeli cabinet. To avoid confusion, she is generally referred to as Meir in this chapter.

17. Meir, *My Life,* 77–78.

18. Syrkin, *Golda Meir,* 69–92; Meir, *My Life,* 112–115, and "Woman's Lib—1930" in Golda Meir, *A Land of Our Own: An Oral Autobiography,* edited by Marie Syrkin (New York: G. P. Putnam's Sons, 1973), 43–45.

19. Martin, *Golda,* 62.

20. Meir, "The Goal of Jewish Workers," in *A Land of Our Own,* 52–57.

21. Syrkin, *Golda Meir,* 191.

22. *Ibid.,* 235–243.

23. Meir, *A Land of Our Own,* 94; *Time,* Dec. 8, 1978, 43.

24. Syrkin, *Golda Meir,* 11, 97; Meir, *A Land of Our Own,* 240.

25. Meir, *My Life,* 459–460.

Further Reading

FRASER, NICHOLAS, and MARYSA NAVARRO. *Eva Perón* (New York: W. W. Norton, 1980). The most balanced treatment of her life to date.

MEIR, GOLDA. *My Life* (New York: G. P. Putnam's Sons, 1975). Popular autobiography; gives readers a good look at her personality.

PERÓN, EVA DUARTE DE. *My Mission in Life,* trans. by Ethel Cherry (New York: Vantage Press, 1953). Although much of this book was ghost written for Evita and changed by her husband, it shows how she wished to be seen and also serves as an excellent example of Peronist propaganda.

SYRKIN, MARIE. *Golda Meir, Israel's Leader* (New York: G. P. Putnam's Sons, 1969). Clear, written by a friend a decade before Meir died.

CHAPTER 11

M. K. Gandhi and Ho Chi Minh: Paths to Independence

When you wish to get foreign rulers to leave your country, which approach is best—violent or nonviolent resistance? Could Gandhi's approach have worked elsewhere?

The contrast between these men and their respective challenges is a striking one. Mohandas Karamchand Gandhi (1869–1948) led a large, religiously inspired, nonviolent resistance movement against the British government of India in the 1920s and 1930s. The British ended nearly 200 years of political and economic domination of India peacefully in 1947, in part because of the work of Gandhi and in part because economic conditions at that time dictated a reduction of the "burdens" of empire.

At the same time the British were leaving India, the French were making a desperate military attempt to retain control of the colonial possessions they had held in Indochina since 1885. Ho Chi Minh (1890–1969), communist president of the Democratic Republic of Vietnam established in northern Vietnam in 1945, used violent resistance to defeat the French between 1946 and 1954. The struggle continued in the 1960s when the Americans sent up to half a million troops at one point to Vietnam in support of the anticommunist South Vietnamese government. Ho Chi Minh died before the last American troops left Vietnam in 1973 and before his troops conquered the regime in the south in 1975.

Ho Chi Minh was honored posthumously when the capital of the former South Vietnam, Saigon, was renamed Ho Chi Minh City in 1975. Gandhi lived long enough to see the British leave India and was disappointed with the results. The Indian subcontinent was split into separate Hindu and Muslim nations. Fifteen million people fled in fear in order to relocate themselves in either Hindu India or Muslim Pakistan. Several million died from riots, civil war, and disease. Gandhi saw this as betrayal of at least three of his cherished beliefs: nonviolent action to bring about change, Hindu-Muslim "unity in diversity" in India, and the basic goodness of man. It may be ironic that Ho, who used violence to free his country, died of a heart attack on September 3, 1969, while Gandhi, the man of nonviolence, was assassinated by a Hindu fanatic on January 30, 1948.

Mohandas Gandhi (called the Mahatma or "Great-Souled One" by his followers) saw himself primarily as a moral teacher for whom the political arena was only one of many places where a person should serve Truth.

Ho Chi Minh (born Nguyen Sinh Cung[1]) saw himself primarily as a man struggling for the independence and unification of his country. For him, questions of morality or theory, even those connected with the Marxist philosophy to which he committed himself, were secondary.

Gandhi wanted Indians to achieve political independence and, more important to him, spiritual maturity through the use of *satyagraha*, or "truth-force." He refused aid, especially military aid, from outsiders. Ho, on the other hand, did not hesitate to accept large amounts of military economic aid from both China and Russia in order to battle the French and Americans.

Yet, despite these personal and political differences, Gandhi and Ho Chi Minh had two things in common, both important in any movement against colonial rule. Despite their disclaimers, both were popular, even charismatic[2] leaders. Each became a personal inspiration to those wishing freedom from foreign rule. Second, these men were the first in their respective countries to bring the rural masses into political life through careful, shrewd organization. Gandhi and Ho embodied, respectively, Indian and Vietnamese nationalism. The fact that each did so, while being so different from the other, and living in social and political settings which were quite different, illustrates the adaptability and appeal of modern nationalism.

Little in Gandhi's early life, except his mother's religiosity, suggested he would be the leader he later became. The young Mohandas seemed "to have little ability and less talent." He was shy, afraid of being ridiculed by others, and a "mediocre student."[3]

Gandhi was impressed by his mother's frequent fasts for self-purification, her daily prayer, and strict prohibitions against smoking, drinking, and eating meat. Putlibai's moral influence on her son's life was significant. Even as a boy, young Gandhi was scrupulous about truth. He refused to cheat on a spelling test, even when his teacher gave him permission by pointing to the correct answer on a neighbor's paper (the teacher wanted to impress a visiting British school inspector with his bright students).[4]

Despite his conscientiousness, Gandhi's academic record improved little. His arranged marriage at age thirteen did not help. He was jealous of his wife, Kasturbai, and for a number of years "their life jerked along through a series of tiffs and sulks." By the time he took an entrance examination for Bombay University, his score was 247.5 out of a possible 625.[5] It was also during this time, at age sixteen, that Gandhi had a traumatic experience in association with his father's death. On the night his father died, Gandhi left his father's bedside temporarily to indulge in "animal passion" with his wife. A messenger soon told him that his father had died. In his autobiography, Gandhi recalled this lapse of duty as "a blot I have never been able to efface or forget." To make his guilt feelings worse, Kasturbai was very pregnant at the time, and the child died soon after birth. All this, psychologists tell us, helps explain Gandhi's later decision to abstain from sex altogether. And that decision influenced Gandhi's politics.[6]

But meanwhile Gandhi, with family urging, settled upon the career of a lawyer. Since legal training could be more easily obtained in London, Gandhi set sail for England in September 1888 after getting his mother's permission and taking a vow to stay away from wine, women, and meat while abroad. His wife and young son stayed at home. It was during three years in London, and as a direct result of his vegetarian vow, that Gandhi began to come alive, intellectually and spiritually. He discovered that English vegetarians could argue a case for avoiding meat which was far more logical than his mother's simple religious prohibition. He also discovered the classic Indian religious work, the *Bhagavad-Gita*, in English translation, and encountered a number of Western advocates of Eastern ideas. In short, he began to discover the East through the West, and to create a philosophy of life which tempered Eastern ideas with a Western sense of precisely how to apply those ideas.

Upon returning to India in 1891, Gandhi's new inner determination was revealed as a result of two insults he suffered. On one occasion, he went to a British official in Kathiawar (his home province in western India) to plead on behalf of his brother; when he insisted on presenting a case which the Englishman did not wish to hear, he was unceremoniously thrown out of the office. In April 1893, Gandhi was hired by some Muslims in his home city of Porbandar to do some legal work for their firm in South Africa. Shortly after his arrival in this white-ruled colony, Gandhi was thrown out of a first-class train compartment just because he was "coloured."[7] These two incidents crystallized his desire to become a reformer and fight injsutice.

That fight would keep Gandhi in South Africa until 1914. At first he followed traditional political methods such as collecting names on a petition when the government of the province of Natal tried to deny the vote to Indians.[8] After 1904, however, Gandhi's personal and political style began to change. At that time, he took up communal living on a farm he bought near Johannesburg. Several years later, he adopted (without consulting his wife) the Hindu practice of *brahmacharya*, or complete sexual abstinence. In 1906, Gandhi coined the word *satyagraha*, or "truth-force," to describe a new type of nonviolent resistance to the government with which the Indians tried to stop a Registration Act that would make them second-class citizens.

Satyagraha involves selective nonviolent lawbreaking by large numbers of people. As Gandhi explained this idea, it was not mere pacifism or a clever political tactic. It was rather a way of confronting Truth within yourself by deciding to take a stand on a clear moral issue. It was also a way of forcing your opponent to confront Truth by allowing yourself to be arrested or even beaten after breaking an unjust law. Gandhi believed that such actions could lead to the conversion of one's political opponent and that such conversion was more important than political success or failure. "Satyagraha," he wrote, "postulates the conquest of the adversary by suffering in one's own person."[9]

Although Gandhi's personal philosophy, and especially his belief in satyagraha, was fully formed by the time he returned to India from South Africa in 1914, he was not yet anti-British or even an advocate of Indian independence. He still believed in the British empire and even recruited for the British army in 1918. That would soon change. When the British government refused to restore civil liberties which had been curtailed during the war, Gandhi asked Indians to engage in a kind of economic sitdown strike *(hartal)* and to combine this with selective civil disobedience. The hartal was a success but some outbreaks of violence caused Gandhi to call off the satyagraha campaign in April 1919 and a smaller one planned for 1922. More serious than Indian violence, however, was the killing of 379 unarmed civilians by a British general in Amritsar (troops fired 1650 rounds, and there were 1516 casualties).[10] The Amritsar massacre in 1919 led Gandhi to proclaim a policy of "non-cooperation" with the British government of India. The keynote of this campaign, which urged people to boycott all British goods, honors, and services, including courts, schools, and jobs, was a seven-month tour of the country by Gandhi. During what seemed to some like revival meetings, he urged peasants and others attending his speeches to spin their own clothes and called spinning a "sacrament." Gandhi would then ask people to place any foreign-made clothing they were wearing in a huge pile. Sometimes there were a few naked people in the crowd; always there was a match to light the bonfire. The fires symbolized both Indian economic dependence on the British, and a growing determination to end that dependence.

Gandhi's advocacy of the spinning wheel was most important, however, as a way of communicating with the millions of Indian peasants. Like his adoption of a simple cloth garment instead of European clothes, it was Gandhi's way of identifying with the poor and creating a bridge between the Indian masses and their leaders. While he intended these actions as forms of communal spiritual uplift, there is no doubt that they were also politically astute. Gandhi was the first Indian political leader to cultivate the peasants by living with them and making sure that the political organization he headed (the Indian National Congress) held its annual meetings in rural areas.

By 1929, demands for complete independence from Britain were growing among Indian leaders. Gandhi returned to the headlines by organizing what became known as the Great Salt March. In what history records as his "finest hour," Gandhi walked 241 miles in 24 days, collecting praise from the peasants and a crowd of several thousand. "We march in the name of God," Gandhi said, promising to "give a signal to the nation" when he arrived at the sea. On the beach at Dandi, the Mahatma defied the British rulers of India (who had a monopoly on the production and sale of salt) by picking up a handful of salt from the beach while one of his followers cried, "Hail, Deliverer." It was a moment, in the words of Gandhi's biographer Louis Fischer, which required "imagination, dignity, and the sense of showmanship of a great artist."[11] And it worked. All across India, peasants began defying the British, wading into the ocean, and producing salt. The British, of course, had to arrest them, even though many Englishmen themselves thought the salt monopoly just the sort of silly law that a revolutionary could exploit.

As a result of this protest, Gandhi went to jail where he stayed, off and on, for several years. During this time, he displayed his seriousness as a religious reformer within his own community by undertaking a fast—which almost killed him—to convince Hindus to change their attitude toward the outcasts, or "untouchables." For centuries, these people were considered religiously unclean and fit only for the most degrading chores. Gandhi called them "Harijan," or "Children of God," and wished to see a Hindu change of heart that would result in equality for them. His fast resulted in the beginnings of such a change. Long-term changes were less dramatic, but at the time, no one wanted the death of the Mahatma on his or her conscience.

Gandhi undertook this and other fasts during his life out of love and, like satyagraha, as a way to change the hearts of his opponents. He claimed that he did not fast in order to coerce people to come to terms, and yet that is exactly how most ordinary people saw the situation. Before his death, Gandhi had fasted a total of 138 days, 35 against untouchability, 29 for Hindu-Muslim unity, 28 as penance for some comrade's moral lapse, and 18 in repentance for some violent action committed by others.[12] In this area, as in many others, Gandhi was the "practical idealist," the holy man whom the politicians feared.

If we accept the sincerity of Gandhi's search for Truth, a search which led him to advocate strict nonviolence "in thought, word, and deed," we can appreciate his bitter disappointment during the last months of his life when Hindus and Muslims began to kill one another. Gandhi was not able to hold his people together, but he was still the Mahatma. As he walked through the strife-torn villages, talking and praying from both Hindu and Muslim scriptures, people often did stop fighting—at least temporarily. His last fast in New Delhi brought Hindu and Muslim leaders in India together— again temporarily—several weeks before his death, which was mourned by members of all faiths in India.

Despite his personal disappointments, Gandhi can be congratu- lated on his success in freeing his country from foreign rule, what- ever the problems which followed. It took the Vietnamese, after all, a full generation longer to get the foreigners out after World War II. Of course, they suffered by having the less "liberal" French as their colonial rulers; they were also hindered by the fact that those most able to free Vietnam were communists. This meant that the fight against Vietnamese independence could be turned into an anticom- munist war. That the Vietnamese succeeded in creating an indepen- dent nation-state in southeast Asia is a tribute to Ho Chi Minh, a man who gave himself the following "advice" in a poem written while in a Chinese prison during World War II:

> Without the cold and desolation of winter
> There could not be the warmth and splendor of spring.
> Calamity has tempered and hardened me,
> And turned my mind into steel.[13]

If Gandhi was a man whose adult life was guided by a persis- tent search for Truth and a desire to teach the ways of Truthseeking to others, the life of Ho Chi Minh was dominated from early child- hood by the pride of a revolutionary willing to use whatever means were necessary to free his country from colonial rule. The region where he was born, Nghe Tinh, along the central coast near the Gulf of Tonkin, was famous as a haven for revolutionaries, and Ho's father, Nguyen Sinh Sac, was himself a patriotic dissenter who lost his government job in 1907 for displaying anti-French sympa- thies. Ho's psychological development, like that of Gandhi, was in- fluenced by his relationship with his father, who gave the boy something to revolt against by leading an irresponsible life while Ho was growing up. In particular, Nguyen Sinh Sac once left the ten-year-old Ho at home alone with his mother, who was about to have a child. When Ho's mother died while his father was gone, we can assume the experience might have created psychological ten- sions for the boy.[14] By becoming a nationalist revolutionary, Ho could express his rebellion against his authority-figure father while at the same time remaining true to his father's dislike of the French.

Modern revolutionaries, especially those in poor colonies, usually had to travel abroad to secure part of their training. After attending high school in the city of Hue, Ho taught for a few months before signing on as part of the kitchen crew of a French passenger liner. He spent two years at sea, visiting ports in North Africa, Europe, and even the United States, where he later claimed to have been impressed by the rights enjoyed by citizens of New York's Chinatown. During World War I, Ho lived in London, earning money by working as a gardener, washing dishes, and shoveling snow.[15] From 1917 to 1923, he lived in France, getting to know Frenchmen who were not as brutal as the colonizers he knew in Indochina, and trying to connect his recent experiences as a proletarian [Marxist term for members of the landless urban working class] with his desire for national independence for his people. Ho became a respected member of the French socialist party, founded and edited a newspaper, *La Paria (The Outcast),* and wrote a bitter pamphlet denouncing the economic and human cost of French colonialism, especially in Indochina. An interesting theme of his early articles is his repeated contention that the French were poisoning the Vietnamese by forcing them to use opium and alcohol in order to enrich French business leaders.[16]

While in France, Ho was given a copy of Lenin's "Thesis on the National and Colonial Questions." It convinced him, he wrote later, that only the communists were really serious about freeing colonial peoples. He became a founding member of the French Communist Party and in late 1923 traveled to Moscow. There he studied, wrote articles for *Pravda,* a leading communist paper, and became an active and respected member of the Comintern, an agency established to promote revolutions outside Russia. For the next fifteen years, Ho travelled through Asia organizing revolutionary groups, dodging arrest, and serving as official Comintern spokesman at international meetings. It was also during these years that Ho began to develop his relationship with the peasants. He lived simply among them and, much like Gandhi, stressed the importance of hygiene and education, and got along very well with children. After World War II, Ho cultivated this image of simplicity, especially in dealings with Westerners. One French journalist who interviewed him in 1946 commented on "the disarming gaze of a Franciscan Gandhi." Another French official, who had to work out an agreement with Ho, referred to his "prestige and popularity in the eyes of the people" and added that he had no doubt Ho "had aspirations . . . of becoming the Gandhi of Indochina."[17]

But if Ho wished to suggest a similarity with Gandhi based upon their shared concern for the poor, their popularity, and their determination to put up with hardship (all of which was true), it is also certain that Ho did not want to be a Gandhi. As early as 1922, he had written an article contrasting the brutality of French rule in Indochina with the relative mildness of British rule in India and Ireland. "The Gandhis and the De Valeras [Irish leader] would have long since entered heaven had they been born in one of the French colonies," he wrote. Necessity made Ho Chi Minh less of a spiritual leader of his people and more of a dedicated anticolonialist and nationalist who used communist ideology and skillful organization as the means to his end: a united Vietnam. For Gandhi, both the means (nonviolence) and the end (Truth) were different.

Of course, their enemies were also different. While the British were willing to leave India at the end of World War II, the French, who had been replaced by the Japanese as rulers in Indochina during World War II, wanted to retain their colony after the Japanese left. At the end of the war, Ho's guerrilla forces took control in the north and proclaimed Vietnamese independence. Ho apparently believed that he might be able to convince the French to leave, and he tried to make it easier for them by downplaying his communism. The French, however, refused to end colonial rule and gambled on a war to suppress the Vietminh revolutionaries, as Ho's men were called. They lost. An eight-year struggle ended in 1954 when a major French fortress at Dien Bien Phu was captured by the communists. An agreement that year divided the country, leaving Ho's Democratic Republic of Vietnam in charge in the north and calling for elections in two years to establish a single government for Vietnam. Ho's problems with the French were over; difficulties with the Americans were to follow.

In the final months of World War II, Ho's relations with Americans had been reasonably good. A downed American airman who worked with Ho for several months in 1945 reported that he was "an awfully sweet guy." Ho wrote letters to President Truman in 1945 and 1946, asking for aid against the French, and some Americans believed later that Ho could have developed as an "independent" communist leader such as Marshall Tito did in Yugoslavia.[18]

Truman thought otherwise, opted for a tough line against communists everywhere after 1947, and by 1950 (after the Korean war began) supplied the French with some $4 billion dollars of aid to fight their war in Indochina. By 1954, the United States was paying seventy-eight percent of the French war bill in Vietnam, more than the percentage of external aid Ho was receiving from his Russian and Chinese supporters.[19] Ho Chi Minh's communist-led independence movement became, by the 1950s, the target of American policymakers bent on containing communism in Asia.

This fact, combined with Ho's continued determination to drive out the foreigners and unify the country, perhaps made inevitable the events of the next twenty years. The United States supported a decision to cancel the 1956 elections, which Ho would probably have won, and instead sponsored an anticommunist state, the Republic of Vietnam, in the southern half of the country. Within a few years, Ho's government was supplying communist-led guerrillas operating in the south (the Viet Cong). Although the government of South Vietnam remained weaker than the one in the north, the weight of American military power, applied through bombing of North Vietnam and large-scale American troop deployments in the south after 1965, was sufficient to delay a final victory by Ho's troops until 1975. Faced with widespread domestic protests against the war and a substantial death toll in a guerrilla war against an elusive enemy, the American government withdrew its troops from Vietnam in 1973.

Ho Chi Minh combined nationalism with communist ideology. Whether that made his struggle for independence and unification of his country more difficult or easier after 1945 is difficult to say. Aid from other communist countries helped him sustain his struggle; yet, had he not been a communist, he might have avoided a long struggle with the Americans. Of course, had the French been less intransigent, he might not have seen communism as the best response to colonial exploitation.

Mohandas K. Gandhi combined his nationalism with a search for moral truth for himself and his people. Whether that made his struggle against the British longer or shorter, harder or easier, is also difficult to know. Gandhi could have called for a full-scale war of independence against the British in 1922 or 1931 after the salt tax protests. Because such a conflict would certainly have been violent, Gandhi refused to approve such a struggle. He withdrew on both occasions, to jail or to his ashram, until such time as the people would be spiritually more mature and able to practice satyagraha wholeheartedly. That day never came. When the British finally left peacefully in 1947, Hindus and Muslims resorted to violence against each other to achieve their respective national goals.

It is intriguing to ask what might have been: Had Ho tried nonviolence, had Gandhi accepted violence, had Ho not been communist, had the Americans not been so anticommunist, had ruthlessness against opponents been a sustained instead of an incidental British policy in India?

Regardless of their considerable differences, these two men were genuine national leaders. Despite talk of a "shrinking world" in our century, our planet is large and culturally varied enough for men to respond to satyagraha in one part of Asia and to sustained guerrilla warfare in another. On one thing people of differing convictions in these countries and elsewhere in the world can agree: However well or badly the Indians or Vietnamese are behaving these days, they are behaving that way on their own. The age of imperialism is over.

Notes

1. For a list of Ho Chi Minh's twenty aliases, including information on when and where he used each, see James Pinckney Harrison, *The Endless War: Fifty Years of Struggle in Vietnam* (New York: Free Press/Macmillan, 1982), 38. To simplify matters, he will simply be called Ho Chi Minh (He Who Enlightens) throughout this chapter.

2. While this word has a specific religious meaning, it is used here in its social-political sense, as "that spiritual power or personal quality that gives an individual influence or authority over large numbers of people." See *Random House Dictionary of the English Language,* Unabridged (New York: Random House, 1967), 248.

3. Louis Fischer, *Gandhi: His Life and Message for the World* (New York: Mentor, 1954), 9–10.

4. Geoffrey Ashe, *Gandhi* (New York: Stein and Day, 1968), 6–7.

5. Ashe, *Gandhi,* 9, 14.

6. Mohandas K. Gandhi, *An Autobiography: The Story of My Experiments with Truth* (Boston: Beacon Press, 1957), 30–31; see E. Victor Wolfen-

stein, *The Revolutionary Personality: Lenin, Trotsky, Gandhi* (Princeton: Princeton University Press, 1967), 73–88; Erik H. Erikson, *Gandhi's Truth: On the Origins of Militant Nonviolence* (New York: W. W. Norton, 1960).

7. Gandhi, *Autobiography,* 97–99, 111–112; at about the time Gandhi arrived, the South African provinces of the British empire were ruled by 600,000 whites outnumbered by 2 million blacks and 65,000 Indians. See Fischer, *Gandhi: Life and Message,* 22–25.

8. Ashe, *Gandhi,* 59.

9. *Ibid.,* 100–103; M. K. Gandhi, *Satyagraha in South Africa,* trans. from the Gujarati by V. G. Desai, Revised Second Edition (Ahmedabad, India: Navajivan Publishing House, 1950), 102–107, 113–114.

10. Fischer, *Gandhi: Life and Message,* 66.

11. *Ibid.,* 98–99.

12. T. K. Mahadevan, *Gandhi My Refrain: Controversial Essays: 1950–1972* (Bombay: Popular Prakashan, 1973), 196.

13. Ho Chi Minh, *The Prison Diary of Ho Chi Minh,* trans. by Aileen Palmer, introduction by Harrison E. Salisbury (New York: Bantam, 1971), 28.

14. Jean Lacouture, *Ho Chi Minh: A Political Biography,* trans. from the French by Peter Wiles (New York: Random House, 1968), 6–15; David G. Marr, *Vietnamese Anticolonialism, 1885–1925* (Berkeley: University of California Press, 1971), 254–255.

15. Lacouture, *Ho Chi Minh,* 17–20; Bernard Fall, *The Two Viet-Nams: A Political and Military Analysis,* Second Revised Edition (New York: Frederick A. Praeger, 1967), 85; Charles Fenn, *Ho Chi Minh: A Biographical Introduction* (New York: Charles Scribner's Sons, 1973), 26.

16. Ho Chi Minh, *On Revolution: Selected Writings, 1920–1966,* edited with an introduction by Bernard Fall (New York: Frederick A. Praeger, 1967), see 68–123 for his pamphlet on French colonialism and his references to opium and alcohol on 4, 19, 69, 76–79, 144.

17. Lacouture, *Ho Chi Minh,* 124–126; see also 148, 175, 217.

18. Robert Shaplen, "The Enigma of Ho Chi Minh," *The Reporter* (January 1955), 11–13; Harrison, *The Endless War,* 92, 97; Fenn, *Ho Chi Minh,* 84; Bernard Fall, *Viet-Nam Witness, 1953–1966* (New York: Frederick A. Praeger, 1966), 7–8.

19. Harrison, *Endless War,* 117.

Further Reading

FISCHER, LOUIS. *Gandhi: His Life and Message for the World* (New York: New American Library, 1954). Short, easy to read. A major film was based on this work.

GANDHI, M. K. *Selected Writings,* Selected and Edited by Ronald Duncan (New York: Harper and Row, 1972). Best short collection.

HARRISON, JAMES PINCKNEY. *The Endless War: Fifty Years of Struggle in Vietnam* (New York: Macmillan/Free Press, 1982). Good overall picture of this long, complicated conflict.

LACOUTURE, JEAN. *Ho Chi Minh: A Political Biography* (New York: Random House, 1968). An insider's account, interesting and readable.

CHAPTER 12

Teller and Sakharov: Scientists in Politics

What are the political implications of major technological developments? How did the careers of these two "fathers of the H-bomb" differ, and what does this tell us about their respective societies?

It was early on the morning of July 16, 1945. The first atomic bomb had just been detonated in the New Mexico desert. After congratulating themselves on the success of the test, the American scientists boarded the bus which would take them back to their laboratory at Los Alamos. One of them, Edward Teller, turned to take a last look. "The desert winds had shaped the mushroom cloud into a giant question mark."[1]

That question mark, which began our age of nuclear weapons, is an important part of twentieth-century world history. The "small" atomic bombs which destroyed the Japanese cities of Hiroshima and Nagasaki in 1945, bringing World War II to an end, were soon replaced by much larger weapons. In competition with each other between 1951 and 1954, the Soviet Union and the United States each developed "super" bombs, thermonuclear hydrogen weapons. The first hydrogen bomb, or H-bomb, exploded by the United States on October 31, 1952, was twenty-five times more powerful than the atomic bomb dropped on Hiroshima; it destroyed the entire Pacific Island of Elugelab, one mile in diameter.[2]

These developments accelerated the nuclear arms race which lay at the heart of the "cold war" between the Soviet Union and the United States from 1945 to the collapse of the USSR in 1991. This nuclear contest formed the backdrop for all actions on the international political stage. During that period, the original 1945 question mark appeared again and again: in novels and movies about nuclear "holocaust," in the many attempts at disarmament by the "superpowers" since the 1950s, and in the frequent protests against increased stockpiling of nuclear weapons that filled newspapers and television screens from the 1960s through the 1980s.

Given the magnitude of nuclear power, it is not surprising that it is difficult to discuss its possible effects rationally. The problem of nuclear weapons, like all other problems discussed in this book, can be better understood if given a human face. In the case of the H-bomb, the human face is really two faces, those of the American and Russian "fathers of the H-bomb," Edward Teller (born 1908)—the man who first saw the question mark—and his Russian counterpart, Andrei D. Sakharov (1921–1989).

Perhaps it is appropriate that such a crucial development in human history should have two fathers. Both of these men were brilliant physicists. But they were more than that. Following the perfection of an operational, or "deliverable," hydrogen bomb, both Teller and Sakharov increasingly turned their attention to the broader political questions raised by their scientific work. As national heroes for a time, both were in a position, rare for scientists, to give advice to their governments. Both favored a balance in weapons between Russia and the United States as a prelude to disarmament and both pushed for peaceful development of nuclear energy. Otherwise their paths, like their societies, were different. Teller pushed for the development of the H-bomb in order to keep up with the Russians; this made him a hero to most Americans and the subject of a *Time* magazine cover story in 1957. A decade later, Andrei Sakharov began his career as a famous Soviet "dissident" when he publicly criticized the closed society and totalitarian government of the Soviet Union. Until late in his life, his many public statements urging greater democracy within the USSR, freedom of thought, free emigration, and arms reduction made him appear a traitor to the government and many people in the Soviet Union. He was treated as such, lived in "internal exile" in the city of Gorky, guarded by police and kept away from his colleagues and the Western press until freed in December 1986 as part of Premier Mikhail Gorbachev's new policy of "glasnost," or "openness."

Despite their different political careers, Teller's and Sakharov's distinct views on the social responsibility of scientists illuminate the fears which beset those who created the nuclear age. Their lives also shed light on "political" scientists in the United States and the

Soviet Union, the nations which sustained the nuclear arms race for forty-five years.

Edward Teller was born in Budapest, Hungary, to a stable lawyer father and a musician mother who was overprotective to the point of tying a string to Edward and his sister when they went swimming. Although his early genius in mathematics irritated his fellow students, his life was more seriously affected by political disorder in Hungary after World War I. An inept communist government which lasted a year was followed by an antisemitic regime which made it necessary for Teller, a Jew, to leave his homeland in order to succeed as a physicist. The political disorder in Hungary during his youth and his family's suffering at the hands of a communist government in 1919 and again after 1945 helped make him an advocate of "conservative capitalism and a strong military establishment." Years later, he recalled that he "had seen, in Hungary, at least one society that was once healthy go completely to the dogs. I have seen the consequences of a lost war."[3]

During the late 1920s when Teller was studying physics in Germany, men like Albert Einstein, Werner Heisenberg, Max Planck, and Niels Bohr were revolutionizing that science by challenging ideas about matter and energy that had been unquestioned since the work of Isaac Newton in the seventeenth century. In 1934, after teaching for several years in Germany, Teller used a Rockefeller Foundation scholarship to study with Niels Bohr in Copenhagen. There he met George Gamow, who invited the newly married Teller to teach with him at George Washington University in Washington, DC in 1935. There the Tellers settled down to what they thought would be the quiet life of a professor of theoretical physics.[4]

That hope died in January 1939, when American physicists discovered that German scientists had split the atomic nucleus in December 1938. Within months, physicists around the world understood that the center or nucleus of certain atoms could be bombarded with neutrons. This process could lead to a chain reaction, releasing incredible amounts of energy. The trick was to control such a nuclear reaction. Whoever did so first could possess a weapon of immense destructive force. At this time, Germany was ruled by Adolf Hitler, and World War II was only months away.

All of this impelled leading American physicists, many of them refugees from Nazi Germany, to push the American government into a serious program of atomic research. After initial disinterest on the part of the military, a famous letter from Albert Einstein to President Franklin Roosevelt stimulated the beginning of an American effort to produce a nuclear chain reaction. After America entered World War II this effort, known as the Manhattan project, accelerated and on December 2, 1942, the first "sustained nuclear chain reaction" was achieved in a laboratory under the football stadium at the University of Chicago.[5] From then on, it was only a matter of time until the first bomb was created in 1945.

The tension between science and politics appeared in Edward Teller's life during these years in the form of two issues. The first was the decision of President Truman to use the new bomb against Japanese cities in order to end the war more quickly and to impress the Soviet Union with US power. In the summer of 1945 some scientists began to circulate a petition asking that the bomb not be used without first warning the Japanese. Teller and some others who favored a demonstration project rather than a drop on a population center refused to circulate the petition at Los Alamos. He had checked with his boss, J. Robert Oppenheimer, who told Teller that he did not think scientists should make "political pronouncements." In a letter to Leo Szilard, the friend who had asked him to circulate the petition, Teller consoled himself by writing that perhaps "actual combat-use" of this terrible new weapon might be the best way to get the facts about nuclear power to the people, who were the ones—in a democracy—who should control its use. In the same letter, Teller suggested scientists were not responsible for political decisions when he wrote: "I feel that I should do the wrong thing if I tried to say how to tie the little toe of the ghost to the bottle from which we just helped it escape."[6] This point he would repeat in the years to come.

A second, more strictly scientific issue which soon involved Teller directly in politics was the possibility of building the "super," or hydrogen, bomb. As early as 1941, he had become fascinated with the idea of capturing the energy of the sun by creating a chain reaction through "fusion" [creating energy by joining several light nuclei to create a heavier nucleus] rather than "fission" [the process of splitting the nucleus used in atomic weapons]. Work on this new, super weapon was opposed by Oppenheimer and most other physicists at the end of World War II. They believed that it would be many years before any other country could develop atomic weapons; Teller alone was realistic about the USSR. He was motivated not by any inside information about the state of Soviet science but by his intense personal distrust of communism. He was proved right when the Soviets exploded their first atomic bomb—called "Joe One" by the Americans—in 1949. Even after that, scientists advising the Atomic Energy Commission (AEC) recommended against work on a hydrogen bomb, urging moral considerations. Teller pushed the project with the help of Lewis Strauss, member and later chairman of the AEC, and Senator Brien McMahon, chairman of the Joint Congressional Committee on Atomic Energy. It was not until January 31, 1950, that President Truman instructed the AEC to "continue its work on all forms of atomic weapons, including the so-called hydrogen or super bomb."[7] Teller was not only the principal scientific inventor of the hydrogen bomb but also the man whose political activities pushed the American government to develop it. For both of these reasons, he is rightly seen as the "father" of the American H-bomb. After J. Robert Oppenheimer, the man who had chaired the General Advisory Committee which recommended against the H-bomb project, lost his security clearance in 1954 because of past association with communists and errors of judgment which frightened many people during the cold war, Teller became a hero to many Americans. He "hurried the H-bomb," in the words of *Newsweek; Life* magazine embarrassed him by calling the project "Dr. Edward Teller's Magnificent Obsession."[8]

Although he claimed to dislike the publicity which followed his scientific success, Edward Teller thrust himself into the spotlight repeatedly over the next forty years. His public comments have been lonely and controversial ones, ranging from his statement at the 1954 Oppenheimer security hearings that he did not fully trust Oppenheimer, to his 1983 support of President Reagan's plan for a missile defense system for America based on laser and particle-beam technology.[9] Both of these positions, and quite a few he took in between, including his opposition to the 1963 treaty banning nuclear tests in the atmosphere, earned him the enmity of most fellow scientists, who tended to be much more liberal politically than Teller.

Yet, given Teller's position as a conservative advocate of a strong defense policy, it is interesting that he repeatedly stated that science and politics should be kept quite separate. "The scientist is not responsible for the laws of nature," he wrote in an article addressed to fellow scientists in 1950 urging them to work with him on the hydrogen bomb project. "It is his job to find out how these laws operate. . . . to find ways in which these laws can serve the human will." Teller stressed that it was "not the scientist's job to determine whether a hydrogen bomb should be constructed, whether it should be used, or how it should be used. This responsibility rests with the American public and their chosen representatives."[10]

However, in this same article, Teller added that, speaking "as a citizen," he was sure that President Truman had made the correct decision when he ordered the AEC to build an H-bomb. After all, Teller wrote in a remark that was clearly political, we were in a situation "not less dangerous than the one we were facing in 1939. . . . We must realize that mere plans are not yet bombs, and . . . democracy will not be saved by ideals alone." In other articles written by or about him in the midfifties, Teller returned to his earlier point that scientists have no "special insights into public affairs"; the "person who makes the bombs is not quite the proper person to know what to do with them." Scientists should remain true to the tradition which urged them to "explore the limits of human achievement." Teller was "confident that, whatever the scientists are able to discover or invent, the people will be good enough and wise enough to control for the benefit of everyone."[11]

Over the years, Teller's confidence in the wisdom of the people seemed to diminish and, as it did so, the line—always an ambiguous one—which separated Teller the scientist from Teller the political figure grew dimmer and easier to cross. In 1957 and 1958, he began strongly advocating the peaceful uses of "clean" nuclear energy. In one essay, he tried to dispel growing fears of radioactive fallout from nuclear explosions, comparing the danger from such explosions to the "equivalent of smoking one cigarette every two months." This was something Sakharov disputed at the time as "unsubstantiated" and "propaganda." By 1968, Teller and other scientists working on "Project Plow-share" had devised many industrial and scientific uses for nuclear explosives. These included geothermal heat production, mining, canal building, and even the construction of highways.[12] Perhaps Teller's opposition to the nuclear test-ban treaty of 1963 indicated most clearly that he was not, in the final analysis, willing to trust "the people" to be "good enough and wise enough" to control nuclear weapons in ways he believed best. "If we renounce nuclear weapons, we open the door to aggression," he stated flatly in 1958. At the congressional hearings on the treaty in the summer of 1963, he went further, calling the test-ban treaty "possibly a step toward war," because it would reduce America's defense against a missile attack—an area in which he was convinced the Russians were ahead.[13]

Teller's sympathetic biographers tell us that while he has been universally respected as a scientist, his performance in the "political theater, where he has been pursuing his scientific goals," finds the audience divided, some cheering and some booing. But Edward Teller pursued not only scientific goals in the political arena, as he did to get the H-bomb built, but also political goals in the political arena. Some of these, such as particle-beam technology, require scientific work. Teller's apparent difficulty in taking his own advice to make "clear-cut distinctions" between scientific and political questions might account for the fact that he remained, according to his biographers, "a strangely restless and vaguely unhappy man, seemingly traveling about the earth in the quest of some elusive and formless Holy Grail."[14]

The "Holy Grail" [this term refers to the cup Christ used at the Last Supper; it was the object of knightly quests in medieval literature and has come to refer to any object of a lengthy search] which Edward Teller sought might be a world in which scientific and political goals rest in harmony, a world in which scientists and political leaders from all countries work together to create a peaceful, prosperous planet. Teller's support at the end of World War II for an end to secrecy and for an international control agency for atomic weapons and research suggests this as his goal. If so, his Russian counterpart, Andrei Dmitriyevich Sakharov, was in full agreement. Sakharov's courageous and persistent conflict with the Soviet government for over fifteen years made him a near-martyr to the cause of human freedom in a totalitarian society. The fact that his political activity pleased liberal intellectuals as much as Teller's dismayed them makes it difficult to see some of the similarities between the views of these two men. At the very least, both were fully aware of how modern science is closely tied to the very unscientific judgments of politicians.

A year before his death, Andrei Sakharov was called "the most admired man of science since Einstein" but also "the conscience of the Soviet people" and "a folk hero for the times."[15] His career began with much less fanfare. A "thin, blond, shy" student, Sakharov graduated from the University of Moscow in 1942 with a record of scientific achievement good enough to exempt him from the army at a time when the USSR was still reeling from Hitler's attack begun a year earlier. For the rest of the war, Sakharov worked as an engineer at a large arms factory where his inventions increased arms production. From 1945 to 1947, this son of a physics teacher and piano player did graduate work in physics at the Lebedev Physical Institute in Moscow, earning a doctorate before being assigned in 1948 to the research group which would develop thermonuclear weapons.

"I found myself," Sakharov recalled some twenty-five years later, "in an extraordinary position of material privilege and isolated from the people." For his top secret weapons research in Turkmenia, Sakharov was paid the equivalent of $27,000 annually, high even in the USA in the early 1950s. He was also given special bodyguards and a chauffeur as well as access to special food and housing. All of this must have been heady wine for a scientist in his twenties who was convinced his work was "essential" to protect his country and to establish a worldwide military equilibrium. Sakharov's work was successful. He was largely responsible for the fact that the first Russian thermonuclear device was exploded several months before that of the Americans.[16]

Sakharov's key role in the development of the H-bomb earned him further awards. He was elected a full member of the Soviet Academy of Sciences in 1953, an honor unprecedented for one his age. On three other occasions, he was awarded the title of "Hero of Socialist Labor." Despite these honors, Sakharov became increasingly troubled by some of the moral implications of his work. He noticed that many of the people with whom he worked were talented but cynical, and his uneasiness was increased by an incident in 1955. Following a successful H-bomb test that year, a banquet was held for the officials. Sakharov proposed a toast that "our handiwork would never explode over cities." A general who was director of the test replied that how a weapon is used is no business of the scientists; the same message was delivered to Sakharov in person by Russian Premier Khrushchev at another banquet in 1961. In 1962 Sakharov tried to stop an atmospheric thermonuclear test that he knew was of no scientific value but that could cause harmful fallout. He failed and said he never got over "the feeling of impotence and fright that seized me on that day." Unlike Teller, Sakharov was very concerned with the danger posed by fallout from tests. He wrote an essay in 1959 expressing concern about the effects of radiation, especially in causing genetic damage. Sakharov suggested some of the provisions of the 1963 test-ban treaty, the same one Teller opposed so strongly in the United States.[17]

It took over ten years for Andrei Sakharov's discontent with the Soviet political system to bloom into full, public dissent. When it did, however, he became a prophet of "perestroika" nearly twenty years before Mikhail Gorbachev introduced this term in the late 1980s to describe his policy of "restructuring" of the Soviet system. In 1968 Sakharov's essay on "Progress, Co-existence, and Intellectual Freedom" was published in *samizdat* form [illegal manuscripts circulated in typescript] in the Soviet Union. It was published in the West after a Dutch correspondent in Moscow read the entire essay over the phone in order to smuggle it out.[18] This work made him famous in the West but lost him his right to work on further secret scientific projects in the USSR. In it Sakharov linked scientific questions such as the "enormous destructive power" of nuclear weapons and "pollution of the environment" to the need for peaceful coexistence and more openness in the Soviet Union. Sakharov initially remained loyal to socialism, calling it the system which has done the most to "glorify the moral significance of labor." Yet he also spoke for "convergence" of the capitalist and socialist systems of government and economy as the basis for peace. Such an agreement or "detente" between the two camps would require greater democracy within the Soviet Union. Sakharov specifically suggested greater intellectual freedom in the USSR, free elections, and even (gradually) a genuine multiparty political system. If this happened the United States and the USSR could use money saved from the arms race to feed and clothe those in poorer nations.

The leaders of the Soviet Union at that time spurned his advice. In 1970, with two other academicians, Sakharov wrote a letter to state and Communist Party leaders urging a freer flow of information, amnesty for political prisoners, and greater democracy and competition in political and economic life. That same year, Sakharov and two other dissidents formed the Moscow Human Rights Committee, a group which appealed to the government on behalf of political prisoners. They especially tried to help those intellectuals forced into psychiatric hospitals for their political statements. Sakharov's "Memorandum" to Communist Party Chairman Leonid Brezhnev in March 1971 asked for "a dialogue with the country's leadership and a frank and public discussion of problems of human rights." In addition to pleas for greater political and economic freedom, this statement also requested prison reform, an end to the death penalty, improved education and medical care, a fight against alcoholism in the USSR, and a change in the Soviet legal system to allow republics within the Union of Soviet Socialist Republics to secede if they wished.[19]

By 1972, relations between Soviet leaders and their brilliant physicist were understandably getting a bit prickly. To make the point that they considered his remarks unwise at best and treasonous at worst, they sent a few signals. His stepdaughter was expelled from the University of Moscow in her senior year. Sakharov himself was harassed by anonymous telephone calls and threats and in March 1973 was summoned to the office of the secret police for a chat. Sakharov's response to this was to allow himself to be interviewed by a Swedish radio correspondent in July 1973. In this interview, he expressed doubts about the wisdom of socialism itself but denied that he wanted to "reorganize the state" or see a revolution, favoring a gradual change to avoid "the terrible destruction through which we have passed several times."[20] This interview was followed by a further official warning to Sakharov and a systematic press campaign against him in August and September 1973. Finally, forty members of the Soviet Academy of Sciences, a group considered somewhat immune to political pressure, signed a statement calling their colleague a "tool of enemy propaganda against the Soviet Union."[21]

While this particular attack on Sakharov ended soon after the president of the American Academy of Sciences intervened on his behalf, neither Sakharov nor the Soviet government immediately changed their minds about each other. During the next six years until 1980, Sakharov continued to speak out on behalf of "prisoners of conscience" in the USSR, often writing letters to Westerners, including one to US President Jimmy Carter in 1977, which included long lists of those imprisoned. More important, Sakharov continued to regard nuclear war as "the greatest danger threatening our age" and in his 1975 Nobel Peace Prize lecture he proposed—much as

Teller had done thirty years earlier—an international agency to effect disarmament and control the spread of nuclear weapons.[22] Sakharov also continued to link disarmament with human rights. Only a freer, more informed public in the USSR could put pressure on the government to act more responsibly in military and foreign policy, he wrote in 1978. The lack of freedom for citizens of the USSR was not just an "internal matter" for him but rather "a menace to international security."[23]

Unwilling to accept this view or to be further embarrassed by this man who was too well known to be shot, the Soviet government, on January 22, 1980, formally stripped Andrei Sakharov of his medals and awards and exiled him to the city of Gorky, where he was closely watched and kept from attending scientific meetings or associating with foreigners for six years. He was released from internal exile on December 16, 1986, informed of this by a personal phone call from President Gorbachev. During the remaining three years of his life, Sakharov was elected to the governing body of the Soviet Academy of Sciences and to the USSR's newly created Congress of Peoples' Deputies, where he served as a leader of the more democratic or radical wing.[24] He also visited the United States in November 1988, where he finally met Edward Teller at a dinner honoring the American physicist. At this meeting, the two men agreed on the wisdom of placing nuclear reactors underground for safety and on the need for openness in political and scientific matters. They disagreed on the value of the American plans to build a space-based missile defense system (SDI or Strategic Defense Initiative), something Teller defended but Sakharov opposed as a "grave error."[25]

Now that the Soviet Union has collapsed, Sakharov's earlier positions on Soviet domestic reform, urging such things as the right to strike, free emigration, and "the right of Soviet republics to secede," seem prophetic rather than naive—as they would have appeared even in 1985.[26] This is perhaps due less to Sakharov's foresight than to the persistence with which Gorbachev pursued his reform of Soviet society and government in the late 1980s.

On the issue of nuclear power and disarmament, Sakharov was often as conservative as his American colleague Teller. In a 1978 essay, Sakharov expressed his support for nuclear power plants, pointing out that the Soviet Union would love to exploit energy shortages in the West. He even repeated Teller's earlier warning against "unfounded emotions and prejudices" in the discussion of nuclear energy. On the issue of disarmament, Sakharov repeatedly asked Western liberals during the 1970s not to be satisfied with a "false detente, a collusion-detente, or a capitulation-detente." They should be wary of unilateral disarmament or of anything less than strict parity in arms reduction. In 1983, Sakharov smuggled a statement out of the Soviet Union stating his opposition to a nuclear freeze and endorsing President Reagan's decision to build 100 MX missiles to counter the Soviet superiority in silo-based intercontinental ballistic missiles (ICBMs).[27]

Neither of these scientists-turned-political-activists fully fit the stereotype which many wished to impose upon them. Teller's support for a "world-wide government to which all owe allegiance and which guarantees freedom," expressed as late as 1962, did not please his conservative supporters any more than Sakharov's support for American arms buildup to achieve "strategic parity" with the USSR pleased the antinuclear movement in Europe or the United States.[28] That is one of the problems we encounter with intellectuals in politics; they are not always predictable.

Edward Teller said that scientists had no special political wisdom, and yet was quite willing to engage in political debates, winning some major political battles in his career. Andrei Sakharov, by contrast, believed scientists do have a "social responsibility." They could not fail, in his view, "to think about the dangers stemming from uncontrolled progress, from unregulated industrial development, and especially from military application of scientific achievements." Until the end of his life, Sakharov won only a few battles in his struggle with the government of the USSR. Yet he exhibited great integrity in fighting, as he put it, "to preserve peace and those ethical values which have been developed as our civilization evolved."[29]

Despite the end of the cold war between the USA and the USSR, the question of nuclear dangers—whether in the form of power plant reactors or warheads on missiles—remains to bedevil us as we approach a new century. The struggle for a peaceful, uncontaminated world is not over; it is only entering another stage. Thanks to Edward Teller, Andrei Sakharov, and the Western desire to explore the limits of the unknown, we continue to live and work in the shadow of the thermonuclear question mark.

Notes

1. Edward Teller with Allen Brown, *The Legacy of Hiroshima* (London: Macmillan and Co., 1962), 18.
2. Stanley A. Blumberg and Gwinn Owens, *Energy and Conflict: The Life and Times of Edward Teller* (New York: G. P. Putnam's Sons, 1976), 295.
3. *Ibid.*, 4–10, 15–27; "Knowledge Is Power," *Time*, Nov. 18, 1957, 22.
4. Blumberg and Owens, *Energy and Conflict*, 28–63.
5. *Ibid.*, 95–122; see also Robert Jungk, *Brighter Than a Thousand Suns: A Personal History of the Atomic Scientists*, trans. by James Cleugh (New York: Harcourt, Brace and Company, 1958), 78–86.
6. Blumberg and Owens, *Energy and Conflict*, 153–163; Teller, *The Legacy of Hiroshima*, 13–15.
7. Blumberg and Owens, *Energy and Conflict*, 185–187, 199–214, 221, 230–231.
8. Harold Lavine, "H-Mystery Man: He Hurried the H-Bomb," *Newsweek*, Aug. 2, 1954, 23–26; Robert Coughlan, "Dr. Edward Teller's Magnificent Obsession," *Life*, Sept. 6, 1954, 60–74. Teller's embarrassment is noted by Blumberg and Owens, *Energy and Conflict*, 369.
9. Blumberg and Owens, *Energy and Conflict*, 362–363; *New York Times*, Mar. 25, 1983, 8; "The Old Lion Still Roars," *Time*, Apr. 4, 1983, 12.
10. Edward Teller, "Back to the Laboratories," *Bulletin of the Atomic Scientists*, March 1950, 71.
11. *Ibid.*, 72; Coughlan, "Teller's Magnificent Obsession," *Life*, Sept. 6, 1954, 67; Lavine, "H-Mystery Man," *Newsweek*, Aug. 2, 1954, 25; Edward Teller, "The Work of Many People," *Science*, Feb. 25, 1955, 275.
12. Edward Teller and Albert L. Latter, *Our Nuclear Future . . . Facts, Dangers and Opportunities* (New York: Criterion Books, 1958), 116–126, 152–159, 167; A. D. Sakharov, *Memoirs*, trans. by Richard Lourie (New York: Alfred A. Knopf, 1990), 203–204; Edward Teller et al., *The Constructive Uses of Nuclear Explosives* (New York: McGraw-Hill, 1968).
13. "Chief Opponent of Test-Ban Treaty: A Man Who Challenges the President" and "Another Round in the Test-Ban Debate," *U.S. News and World Report*, Sept. 2, 1963, 12, 52–57.
14. Blumberg and Owens, *Energy and Conflict*, 1, 450.
15. Irwin Goodwin, "Changing Times: Sakharov in the US on Human Rights and Arms Control," *Physics Today* (February 1989), 91.
16. A. D. Sakharov, *Sakharov Speaks*, edited by Harrison E. Salisbury (New York: Alfred A. Knopf, 1974), 5, 167; Sakharov, *Memoirs*, 97. The first-hand autobiographical information on Sakharov in this work can be supplemented by "An Autobiographical Note" by Sakharov and "Some Events in the Scientific and Public Careers of Andrei D. Sakharov," in *On Sakharov*, edited by Alexander Babyonyshev (New

York: Knopf Vintage, 1982), xi–xxix. For the sequence of the Russian and American explosions and the secrecy surrounding them, see Blumberg and Owen, *Energy and Conflict,* 267–270.

17. A. D. Sakharov, *My Country and the World,* trans. by Guy V. Daniels (New York: Alfred A. Knopf, 1975), 73–74, 33–34; *On Sakharov,* 175–177.
18. Sakharov, *My Country and the World,* viii–ix; *Progress, Coexistence and Intellectual Freedom,* with an "Introduction" and "Afterword" by Harrison E. Salisbury (New York: W. W. Norton, 1968).
19. *Sakharov Speaks,* 116–150.
20. *Ibid.,* 50, 166–178.
21. *Ibid.,* 180–192; George E. Munro, "The Case of A. D. Sakharov," *Midwest Quarterly,* Volume 20, Winter 1979, 147–159.
22. A. D. Sakharov, *Alarm and Hope,* edited by Efrem Yankelevich and Alfred Friendly, Jr. (New York: Alfred A. Knopf, 1978), 43–56, 5–12.
23. *Ibid.,* 99–105, 173.
24. See "On Accepting a Prize" by Sakharov in *New York Review of Books,* Aug. 13, 1987, 49; "On Gorbachev: A Talk with Andrei Sakharov," *New York Review of Books,* Dec. 22, 1988, 28–29; "Sakharov in US Puts in Plug for Perestroika" and "Sakharov Ought to Know," *Christian Science Monitor,* Nov. 8, 1988, 3, 13.
25. Goodwin, "Changing Times: Sakharov in the US," 91–96; *Ethics and Public Policy Center Newsletter* (December 1988), 1, 3.
26. Sakharov, *My Country and the World,* 101–103.
27. Sakharov, *Alarm and Hope,* 124–128; *Sakharov Speaks,* 54; *My Country and the World,* 85–98; "A Plea for Nuclear Balance," *Time,* July 4, 1983, 15–16.
28. Teller, *The Legacy of Hiroshima,* 313.
29. A. D. Sakharov, "The Social Responsibility of Scientists," in *Physics Today,* June 1981, 25–30.

Further Reading

BLUMBERG, STANLEY, AND GWINN OWENS. *Energy and Conflict: The Life and Times of Edward Teller* (New York: G. P. Putnam's Sons, 1976). Honest yet critical biography. Best available.

SAKHAROV, A. D. *My Country and the World,* trans. by Guy V. Daniels (New York: Alfred A. Knopf, 1975). These essays clearly show how Sakharov's hopes anticipated future changes in the USSR.

SAKHAROV, A. D. *Sakharov Speaks,* edited with an introduction by Harrison E. Salisbury (New York: Alfred A. Knopf, 1974).

TELLER, EDWARD L., AND ALBERT LATTER. *Our Nuclear Future . . . Facts, Dangers and Opportunities* (New York: Criterion Press, 1958). Shows early scientific optimism about the potential peaceful uses of nuclear power.